AN ILLUSTRATED TREASURY OF

Bible Stories

VOLUME TWO

AN ILLUSTRATED TREASURY OF

Bible Stories

Retold by Owen S. Rachleff

ABRADALE PRESS *PUBLISHERS* NEW YORK

Standard Book Number: 8109-0192-7
Library of Congress Catalogue Card Number: 71-82034
Published in the United States of America, by
ABRADALE PRESS, INC., NEW YORK

CONTENTS

VOLUME ONE

VOLUME TWO

Stories from the Acts of the Apostles, and the Epistles

The Revelation of St. John the Divine

AN ILLUSTRATED TREASURY OF

Bible Stories

THE BOOKS OF

JEREMIAH

AND THE

LAMENTATIONS

The Story of Jeremiah's Prophecies;
of the Fall of Judah and the Captivity of the Jews.

Jeremiah

NEBUCHADNEZZAR WAS the true master of Judah, for King Jehoiakim was weak, and did as his Babylonian master commanded. Once again, the people turned to idol worship.

In a small town near Jerusalem, there was a good man who had been born during the times of King Josiah. Though the son of poor, hard-working people, he was to become one of the greatest prophets of the Lord. His name was Jeremiah, and in his soul there was a passion for justice, and a sorrow for the sad condition of his nation.

Jeremiah grew up a lonely and shy young man. But, when King Jehoiakim came to the throne and the Babylonians entered Jerusalem, Jeremiah took courage and went out to preach.

At first, no one listened to the youthful prophet, who was timid and unsure of himself. But as time went on, the Lord strengthened his heart and gave him wisdom and strength.

With new determination, Jeremiah went to the Temple of Jerusalem and climbed to the top of the high marble staircase. There he called to the people below, and said:

"Turn from your wicked ways, or the kingdom of Judah will surely perish!"

There was no response; the people merely shrugged their shoulders and walked away. Feeling that he had failed, Jeremiah decided to dramatize his words, and he placed on his shoulders a heavy wooden yoke, such as oxen wear in the fields. Again he came before the people.

"Unless you turn to God," he cried, "our enemies will place the yoke of slavery upon our people even as this yoke is on my back today."

But everyone merely laughed at the sight, and ignored the prophet.

Time after time, Jeremiah tried to warn the people of their doom. One day, he brought a sack of pots and dishes to the Temple. Standing before the crowd, he smashed the dishes against the wall and shouted:

"Our people will be dispersed like the shattered pieces of a broken plate, unless we turn away from wrongdoing."

The Books of Jeremiah and the Lamentations

The people thought that Jeremiah was insane, and, again, they laughed and turned away. But the brave prophet of God kept on. He stood in the doorway of the Temple and stopped the people as they entered.

"Do you think you can wash away your sins," he asked, "just by going to the Temple once in a while? God sees all. He knows our hearts. The humblest man who prays at home is more loved by the Lord than those unbelievers who come to the Temple."

When the soldiers of the king heard this, they arrested Jeremiah for treason. They said that he was preaching against the law of the land. But the princes of the palace were afraid to harm a righteous man. They released him with a warning never to enter the Temple again.

Jeremiah Writes God's Word

ALONE AND WITHOUT FRIENDS, Jeremiah continued his preaching. Then he heard the voice of God:

"I will give you many new laws for the people to obey," said the Lord. "You must write them in a book. I will also prophesy many punishments that will befall the kingdom of Judah. Preach My word to all men, so that they may be saved, for, if the people listen, I will not destroy Jerusalem."

Jeremiah immediately set about to prepare the book of God's Holy Word. He called upon a man named Baruch, who was trained in writing. Through many nights and days, Jeremiah spoke the words of God while Baruch wrote them down.

When the book was completed, Jeremiah told Baruch to bring it to the Temple and read it to all the people assembled there, because Jeremiah himself was no longer allowed to visit the sacred building. Baruch obeyed, and, standing at the head of the great staircase, he read aloud the words of God that foretold the doom of Judah.

When the people heard him, they were angry and afraid.

"Tell us who wrote these terrible words!" they shouted. Baruch admitted that the prophet Jeremiah had written the book.

Some people ran to tell the king, and others, friendly to Baruch, warned him and Jeremiah to hide themselves from the wrath of Jehoiakim.

The king was merely curious about this troublesome book, and he ordered it brought to the palace and read to him. Seated before his roaring fireplace, the king listened while the doom of Judah was read aloud.

"This is miserable nonsense!" he cried. "Give me my knife!" And he took his knife and cut the pages from the book, one by one. Then he hurled them into the fire. He continued to do this until the whole book was burnt. Many people were afraid when they learned of this sacrilege.

Jeremiah was not alarmed. Again, he called upon Baruch, and again he patiently uttered the words of God as Baruch wrote them down.

In spite of this new book the king and the princes paid no attention to the prophet, and continued to live contrary to God's commandments. Then, one day, the great armies of the Chaldeans, under Nebuchadnezzar, marched into the city. They captured the fortress; they ruined the Temple; and they put the king in jail. Through all this misery, Jeremiah begged the people to be brave.

"Even if we are taken as slaves," he cried, "let us not forget our God. Even in captivity we may worship him, for He is all over the world and not just here in Judah."

This was a new idea, and the people didn't understand it. They thought that Jeremiah approved of Nebuchadnezzar's invasion and that he wanted Judah destroyed. Many hated him, and blamed his book for all their troubles. Jeremiah was arrested and put in jail.

When Nebuchadnezzar was victorious, he placed a man on the throne of Judah who would do just as he was told. This man was named Zedekiah, and he was to be the last king of Judah's history. At first, Zedekiah listened obediently to the Babylonian king. But Zedekiah rebelled when Nebuchadnezzar returned to his own land. For a few short years, Judah seemed strong again. Then Nebuchadnezzar decided to teach his enemies a lesson. Once again, he led the great Chaldean army toward Jerusalem.

Fearfully, Zedekiah called for the prophet Jeremiah, and said to him,

"What is to be our fate? Will the Chaldeans be defeated? Answer and say they will not come."

Jeremiah was firm.

"I cannot make up words to please you," he said. "It is the will of God that Judah be destroyed unless the people repent."

Hearing this terrible warning, Zedekiah ordered Jeremiah thrown back into prison.

But, after several months, Jeremiah was freed by friends, and he continued to preach the word of God.

"The enemy is coming!" he announced. "And he will defeat us. Those that remain in this city shall die by the sword, but he who goes forth a captive, he shall live. This is God's plan, and, if we are worthy, some day we can return to Judah as righteous people.

"Therefore, obey the voice of the Lord," he cried, "and peacefully surrender!"

When the king heard that Jeremiah was actually telling the people to surrender and accept captivity, as it was God's will, Zedekiah ordered the arrest of the prophet.

Jeremiah in the Muddy Pit

THE KING'S SOLDIERS captured Jeremiah while he was preaching. Secretly they dragged him to a dungeon and lowered him by a rope into an old well, which was filled with mud. There the great prophet prayed to God, even though surrounded by filth.

But Zedekiah had accomplished nothing by his cruelty to Jeremiah, for Nebuchadnezzar's armies were closing in. It seemed that there was no hope in all the land.

A servant in the king's palace knew of Jeremiah's misery. He was a Negro named Ebedmelech. He went to the king and said:

"Release Jeremiah from the pit, or else he will die."

The king did not desire his death, and he ordered thirty soldiers to remove Jeremiah from the muddy pit. Carefully they raised the prophet by ropes strapped under his arms. When he was cleaned and rested, he was taken before the king.

"It is God's will that Jerusalem shall fall," he said. "But the Lord is merciful, and He will spare the lives of all the people in Judah, your own included, if you do not resist."

Zedekiah didn't know what to do. He kept Jeremiah in the palace under guard, so that the prophet would not excite the people. Then, fearfully, he watched from his window as Nebuchadnezzar's enormous army massed outside Jerusalem, waiting to attack.

Months passed and nothing happened. Every day, the food supply diminished and the people were miserable and hungry. Finally, King Zedekiah decided to escape. But it was to no avail. He crept out of the palace by a secret door, only to find himself sur-

rounded by the enemy. This was all the Chaldeans needed as an excuse to attack. They blinded King Zedekiah, killed his sons, and set fire to the city.

Now Jeremiah rushed to the streets, and cried to the people:

"Surrender and live, so that you may repent in captivity, for it is better to live and worship as a captive abroad than to die here in Jerusalem!"

Many obeyed the prophet and were led away as captives. Others perished as the Chaldeans plundered the city. When the destruction was complete, and the great Temple lay in ruins, only Jeremiah and his Negro friend were allowed to go free.

Thus, after almost 350 years, the great kingdom of Judah was destroyed, as had been prophesied.

The Books of Jeremiah and the Lamentations

The Captivity

WHO HAD BEEN at fault? Surely the people were not entirely to blame. They had been ruled by weak and sinful kings. Now, at last, the kings were gone and a governor named Gedaliah was placed by the Babylonians over the remnants of Judah.

Jeremiah chose to stay behind with those too old or too sick to travel all the way to Babylon. Sitting on the broken walls of the burned-out Temple, he surveyed the ruins of his city and wept. All day and night he wept and he lamented:

> How doth the city sit solitary,
> that was full of people!
> how is she become as a widow!
>   she that was great among the nations,
>   and princess among the provinces,
> how is she become tributary!
> She weepeth sore in the night
>   and her tears are on her cheeks:
> Among all her lovers
>   she hath none to comfort her:
>   all her friends have dealt treacherously with her,
>   they are become her enemies.
> Judah is gone into captivity because of affliction
>   and because of great servitude:
> She dwelleth among the heathen,
>   she findeth no rest.

A few years after the destruction of the Temple, there seemed to be some hope again in the land of Judah. Groups of determined people, led by Jeremiah, began rebuilding the countryside. Gedaliah, the governor, was a kindly man and helped as best he could. But treachery was everywhere. One day, Gedaliah was secretly murdered by men from a neighboring kingdom. When the people learned of this, they were afraid.

"Nebuchadnezzar will put the blame on us," they said. "We must escape."

Jeremiah urged them to be calm.

"Do not run away," he pleaded, "or Judah will surely become a wasteland forever."

But, once again, the people would not listen to their prophet, and, in fear, they fled this way and that, many ending up in Egypt. Jeremiah was taken along to Egypt against his will. There, according to tradition, he was put to death by his detractors.

THE BOOK

OF

EZEKIEL

The Story of Ezekiel's Visions While in Captivity.

The Wonderful Ezekiel

THE KINGDOM OF JUDAH had perished, but the people were still alive. The many thousands taken as prisoners into Babylon came to be known as Jews. They were destined to remain together for two hundred years, even without a country of their own. But their unfortunate neighbors, the Israelites, had vanished completely.

In Babylon, which lay many miles to the east of Canaan, the Jews were strangers. Fortunately, they were treated with kindness by their masters, and, very often, they rose to positions of wealth and dignity.

In spite of this, they kept away from other people because they worshiped the one true God and their Babylonian neighbors worshiped idols. The Jews, in their sadness and in their captivity, had finally become the people of God. But they missed their homeland and often wept:

> If I forget thee, O Jerusalem,
>> let my right hand forget her cunning.
> If I do not remember thee,
>> let my tongue cleave to the roof of my mouth;
>> if I prefer not Jerusalem above my chief joy.

One of the most remarkable Jewish prophets of this time was Ezekiel, who was brought to Babylon during the earliest days of the captivity. He was a man of visions, to whom the Lord spoke in many puzzling ways. Ezekiel was able to predict the fall of Jerusalem and the destruction of the Temple months before the events occurred. How did he know? Here are his words, as he wrote them:

"This is what I saw in the heavens; four creatures, each with wings; and the one had the face of a man, the second the face of a lion, the third the face of an ox, and the fourth was in the likeness of an eagle. And the sky behind these creatures was the color of fire and ice.

"Then they let down their wings and I was lifted up, and they took me away for many miles, and they brought me even to Jerusalem, and the Lord showed me the wickedness of Jerusalem and its abominations."

Ezekiel could also see the armies of Nebuchadnezzar suddenly descending up-

on the city, setting fire to the walls and ruining the sacred Temple. All this he saw in his vision.

The next day, Ezekiel went among the Jews who had just been brought into Babylon. They were sad, and they waited by a river, wondering if they might not have done better to have remained in Judah.

But Ezekiel described his vision and told them that many hundreds would die and that Jerusalem would crumble; even the sacred Temple would be destroyed. He said it was better that they had fled, as Jeremiah had instructed.

Soon after, news came that confirmed all of Ezekiel's predictions. The people knew that a man of God was in their midst. From that time on, they listened when he spoke of his visions.

"I have seen a chariot of fire drawn across the heavens," he said. "There were wheels within wheels, and they all went around and around, as it is God's will that we survive and live and worship Him."

These words gave comfort to the sad and lonely Jews. They asked Ezekiel again and again to tell them of his visions.

"I see a field filled with old, dry bones," he said, "and the Lord commands the dry bones to rise up like men, and soon the bones are covered with flesh, and they become whole again and they breathe and walk and they are revived!"

"What does it mean?" the people wondered.

"We, the Children of Israel, we are like old, dry bones," the prophet said. "We seem hopeless and destroyed. But someday, God will breathe the breath of life back into our nation, and we shall return to our homeland once more.

"Behold," Ezekiel continued. "I have a stick in each hand. One is marked Judah, the other Israel. See, they move together. They have become one by the will of God. This means that our divided nation will join again, and that our people will return to the Holy Land if we are righteous and deserving."

From these wonderful words of Ezekiel, the Jewish captives took hope and comfort for many years. Indeed, they lived to see their enemies crumble—in Egypt, in Philistia, and in Babylon itself. They lived to return briefly to the Holy Land—always under the oppression of a foreign king. And then, in our very own time, within the memory of many people who read this book, Ezekiel's prophecy came true at last, and the nation of Israel was re-established after thousands of years!

The Book of Ezekiel

THE BOOK

OF

DANIEL

*The Story of the Wise Man Daniel, Who Was Thrown
to the Lions and Delivered by God; of the Return to Judah
by the Children of Israel.*

Four Hebrew Boys

KING NEBUCHADNEZZAR WAS the most powerful man in the world. His kingdom extended far and wide. His wealth was very great, and he had many slaves. Nevertheless, Nebuchadnezzar was generous and just. He thus commanded his soldiers to go among the Jewish captives and select a group of strong young men who could be trained to become leaders in Babylon. Nebuchadnezzar was willing to educate these young men in the language of Babylon, and to give them high positions and wealth if they proved qualified.

Four young Jews were selected for this special opportunity. They were brave and handsome. Above all, they were quick to learn; and, soon, they could speak the Babylonian language as easily as their own. Before long, they dressed and talked exactly like Babylonians.

Three of these boys changed their names as well. They became Shadrach, Meshach, and Abednego. The fourth young man was called Belteshazzar, but he refused to give up his Hebrew name.

"I am Daniel," he said, "and that is how I wish to be known." He was so insistent that the king allowed him to keep his Hebrew name.

While Daniel and his three friends were learning the ways of Babylon, they lived in a special house, and every day Nebuchadnezzar sent delicious food for them to eat. Unfortunately, this food was not prepared according to the Laws of Moses, and Daniel would not eat it.

"Bring us lentils to eat and water to drink," he asked the servants of Nebuchadnezzar, "for we do not wish to eat any foods forbidden by our religion."

At first the king's men were afraid to carry out this request.

"If you don't eat properly," they said, "you will grow pale and thin, and the king will hold us responsible."

"Let us try it for ten days," Daniel said. "If we become thin, then we will eat the king's food, and he will never know."

The servants agreed and every day they brought the lentils and the water to the young Hebrews. As the days went by, Daniel and his friends grew stronger and healthier than all those people who ate the Babylonian food. The king's servants were no longer afraid. In fact, they were complimented by Nebuchadnezzar himself for taking such good care of the young Jewish men.

After three years, Daniel and his friends were the best-looking and most intelligent young men in the kingdom. God had given them wisdom and strength, for they worshiped Him alone and never disobeyed His commandments.

Nebuchadnezzar Has a Dream

ONE NIGHT, King Nebuchadnezzar suddenly awoke from his sleep. He had just experienced a very strange dream that had greatly bothered him. Hurriedly, he called his wise men together, so that they might explain its meaning. But then, to his great annoyance, he found he could not remember the dream.

"I want you to discover the meaning of my dream," he said. "It troubles me greatly."

"But how can we interpret your dream, if you have forgotten it?" the wise

men asked. "In all the world, no man can do that."

Nebuchadnezzar would not listen to reason. He sent out an order for all the wise men in Babylon to be executed unless they could discover his forgotten dream.

When Daniel heard of this, he went directly to the king.

"Instead of killing innocent men," he exclaimed, "allow me the chance. If I fail, you may kill me alone. All I ask is a little time to pray."

Nebuchadnezzar agreed, and repealed his order of execution. Then he waited for Daniel.

The young Hebrew meanwhile went to his three friends and urged them to join him in prayer, so that God would reveal the nature of Nebuchadnezzar's dream. After many hours in silent devotion, Daniel exclaimed:

"I know the dream! God has given me the solution."

Then he rushed to the palace and stood before Nebuchadnezzar.

"O, mighty King," he said. "No wise man on earth could tell you what you had dreamed. Only God could do that, and He has seen fit to reveal the secret to me. Now you will know that the God of Israel is the one true God of all the world."

"Yes, yes," said Nebuchadnezzar impatiently, "but tell me my dream."

Daniel continued:

"You have been worried about the future. With this in mind, you went to bed one night and dreamed that you saw what appeared to be a mountainous statue. Its head and shoulders were made of gold and its arms of silver; its body of brass. But its legs were formed of iron, and its feet were partly made of clay."

"Yes," cried the king, "that was my dream! Now you must tell me what it means."

The Book of Daniel

Daniel explained that the statue represented the vast empire of Babylon led by Nebuchadnezzar himself, symbolized by the head of gold. The other nations, which formed his kingdom, were made of either brass or silver. The danger was that the feet that held up this mighty kingdom were merely made of clay. Therefore, in the dream, when a great stone rolled down from heaven and smashed into the statue, it crumbled the feet of clay, and the entire kingdom crashed to the ground, breaking into thousands of tiny pieces. The stone then began to expand; it grew very large, until it had filled the statue's place.

From this, Daniel drew a grave conclusion.

"God is warning you that even your great power will end," he said, "and that His power alone will cover the earth."

Nebuchadnezzar was so amazed by the accuracy of Daniel's description of his dream, and so frightened by the prophecy, that he fell to his knees and exclaimed:

"Daniel, you are a god!"

"No," Daniel insisted. "The one true God of Israel alone was responsible for my revelation. I beg you to rise and give proper thanks to the Lord."

The king agreed. He then bestowed great honors upon Daniel, and also upon Shadrach, Meshach, and Abednego, whom he made governors of his lands. For a time, Nebuchadnezzar actually seemed to believe in the one true God of Israel. But he was to change his mind very rapidly.

The Fiery Furnace

"BUILD A STATUE of me, ninety feet tall, and cover it with gold," commanded Nebuchadnezzar one day. "Then set this statue on the plain of Dura, and there all the people of the kingdom must come and worship me."

When Nebuchadnezzar's subjects heard this strange command, they were fearful, and quickly obeyed. They built the statue, covered it with gold, and set it high on the plain of Dura.

Then the word went forth: "Everyone must fall on his knees before the statue of our king as soon as the trumpets are heard. Anyone who disobeys this command will be burned in a fiery furnace."

Tens of thousands gathered on the plain of Dura to worship the idol of the king. When the trumpets were blown, they fell to their knees and groveled. Even the princes and high officials of Babylon worshiped in this fashion.

Only Shadrach, Meshach, and Abednego refused to bend their knees to an idol made of gold. Their enemies immediately reported the news to the king. Nebuchadnezzar was enraged.

"Is it true," he said to Shadrach, Meshach, and Abednego, "that you refuse to worship my image?"

And they nodded.

"Very well," answered the king, "I will give you one more chance. The next time you hear the royal music, you will bow down to the image on the plain of Dura. If you do not bow down you will be cast into the fiery furnace. Who is that God who can deliver you from my hands?"

"We shall not obey," answered the three young men. "And we will trust in our God to deliver us from your punishment."

"Take them to the furnace and make it seven times hotter," cried the furious king.

Daniel was out of the country at this time, and it seemed as though no one could save the three young men. They were bound with rope and led to the fiery pit. Then, when the heat had become unbearable and the flames leaped higher and higher, Nebuchadnezzar ordered Shadrach, Meshach, and Abednego tossed into the furnace.

"That is the end of them," said the king.

But suddenly the door of the furnace, which had been sealed, swung open wide, and there, in the fiery pit, Nebuchadnezzar could see Shadrach, Meshach, and Abednego walking about unharmed—and with them was another figure in flowing robes.

"Did we not throw three men into the flames?" the king questioned in surprise.

"That is true," his soldiers replied.

"But I see four!" Nebuchadnezzar exclaimed. "One is like an angel, protecting the others, so that they will not burn."

It was true. Shadrach, Meshach, and Abednego were completely safe even in the midst of the flames, and with them was a strange figure who had joined them in prayer.

Nebuchadnezzar was frightened and trembling. He ordered the prisoners removed from the furnace at once, and, when they were brought before him, he could see that not even a hair of their heads had been singed. Only the ropes that bound them had burned away.

"Surely the God of Israel has saved these men," cried the king. "Blessed is the Lord of Shadrach, Meshach, and Abednego. From this day forth, no one may threaten these men or deny them the right to worship their God as they desire. If anyone disobeys, he shall die and his house shall be destroyed."

And then Nebuchadnezzar gave Shadrach, Meshach, and Abednego great gifts and high honors in his kingdom.

The Madness
of Nebuchadnezzar

FOR A LONG TIME, Nebuchadnezzar tried to worship God, but his power and enormous wealth made him boastful and vain. He knew that he was greater than any man in his kingdom, and, soon, he believed himself greater than God. One night, he had a disturbing dream, and he called Daniel to his chamber.

"I dreamed that there was an enormous tree standing in a field," said the king, "and suddenly a voice from heaven commanded, 'Cut down that tree; scatter its branches; and leave only its stump standing for seven years.' Then the tree was cut down and fell to the ground and the voice said, 'God, not man, rules the earth.' What does this mean?"

Daniel was silent for a long time; then he spoke with a heavy heart.

"The Lord is warning you of your downfall, for he will cut you down like a tree, and scatter the branches of your kingdom. Then, for seven years, you will live like a beast in the fields unless you worship Him and lead a godly life."

Nebuchadnezzar was at first alarmed. But, after a time, when he saw that nothing unusual had happened, he became bold again and walked about his palace boasting of his greatness and wealth.

Then, one day, the soldiers in the palace were horrified. There in the fields, on his hands and knees, was the great king Nebuchadnezzar, and he was eating grass and growling like an animal.

"The king has lost his mind," the people cried. "His kingdom has been taken away from him by the will of God."

And so it was for seven years, as Daniel prophesied, that King Nebuchadnezzar lived like a beast in the grass, his hair grown long, his fingernails shaped like claws. No one could tell whether he was a man or a lion.

But, after seven years, God in His mercy restored Nebuchadnezzar's sanity. The king repented and lived a godly life until his death.

The Handwriting on the Wall

WHEN NEBUCHADNEZZAR DIED, his son Belshazzar came to the throne. He had inherited all his father's wealth and power, but none of the respect for God that the old king learned toward the end of his life. So it was that Belshazzar was a fun-loving, sinful king who liked nothing better than big parties and too much wine.

One night, he gave a banquet to which he invited hundreds of wealthy friends. Food and wine were abundant, and the entertainment was splendid, indeed. During the meal, the king and his guests drank and ate from the precious cups and plates that Nebuchadnezzar had taken from the sacred Temple in Jerusalem. Beautiful gold dishes that once held the holy bread of the Temple were now smeared with the unholy food of idol worshipers.

Such a turn of events greatly pleased King Belshazzar, who thought of himself as the most powerful man in the world. Full of merriment, he rose from his throne and held up his goblet of wine.

"I wish to make a toast," he laughed.

But, as he lifted his cup, a cold wind blew through the hall and a strange light filled the room. Belshazzar was alarmed. He turned and looked over his shoulder to see what had happened. There, hovering in mid-air, was a human hand tracing four strange words across the wall in letters of fire.

"*Mene, Mene, Tekel, Upharsin,*" wrote the mysterious hand.

The king was horrified, and fell into his chair.

"What does this mean?" he cried to his guests.

But no one knew. Even the wise men trembled, for they could not offer an explanation; and they tried to sneak out of the room.

"What does it mean?" the king cried again.

Finally, the queen came forward and said:

"Years ago, your father called upon a wise Hebrew named Daniel to interpret his dreams. Perhaps this same man can explain the meaning of the handwriting on the wall."

Belshazzar ordered his soldiers to find Daniel at once.

"If he can tell me the answer," he said, "I will give him fine robes and a chain of gold."

Then the king remained on his throne, afraid and trembling, as the magical words continued to glow on the wall.

When Daniel arrived in the palace, he was brought before the king.

"I have heard that you are a wise man," said Belshazzar. "Very well, tell me the meaning of these glowing words on the wall, and I will make you rich and powerful."

"I don't wish to be rich," Daniel replied. "I shall pray to God, and discover the meaning of these words without reward."

Then Daniel studied the handwriting and said:

"You inherited a great kingdom from your father, but you, Belshazzar, have sinned, and worshiped idols, and you have taken the sacred goblets and plates that were brought from the Temple in Jerusalem and have used them for your unholy food. Therefore, God has sent down His judgment, in these words:

"*Mene*. This means that God has numbered the days of your kingdom and brought them to an end.

"*Tekel*. This means that you have been judged by the Lord and found wanting.

"*Upharsin*. This means that your kingdom will be divided up among the Persians and the Medes. This is God's punishment for all your sins."

Belshazzar was terrified. Nevertheless, he gave Daniel a chain of gold as he had promised, and he appointed him a ruler in the kingdom.

But, even at that moment, God's judgment was being carried out. Outside, all around the city, the great army of Medes and Persians was preparing to attack. At midnight, they charged. When morning dawned, all Babylon had been captured, King Belshazzar was dead, and a man named Darius, from the eastern kingdom of the Medes, was placed on the throne. From that day on, the great empire of the Babylonians belonged to the Persians and the Medes, as Daniel had prophesied.

Daniel in the Lion's Den

DARIUS WAS a noble king who treated his subjects with kindness. He had a special liking for Daniel, whom he considered very wise and very brave. For this reason, the king made Daniel his chief minister, so that the Hebrew was second in command throughout the Persian kingdom. Daniel's high position made many Persian princes jealous, and they began to plot against him.

"We must catch Daniel in a mistake," they said, "so that the king will get rid of him. But, alas! he does no wrong, and we can find nothing against him to report!"

The Book of Daniel

It was true. No matter how they tried, the jealous Persians could not accuse Daniel of any mistakes. They thought up a clever plan, however, and went to the king.

"O mighty Darius," they said, "you are like a god among the people. We believe that everyone in this land should worship you and no other god for thirty days. Anyone who disobeys should be tossed into a den of lions."

King Darius was flattered by this idea, and, after much persuasion, signed the decree making himself a god. Such a decree could not be revoked once it was signed—a fact that the evil Persians knew, for it was their intention to catch Daniel worshiping the one true God of Israel, and, thus, cause him to be thrown to the lions.

Their plan worked well. Daniel would not obey the king's decree, and worshiped God three times a day as he had always done. When they saw this, the wicked Persians rushed to the king with the news.

"Daniel has disobeyed your decree," they cried. "He must be punished."

King Darius was very upset. He admired Daniel, and did not wish to do his friend harm. But the law was the law, and it could not be changed.

Sadly, Darius called Daniel to his chambers.

"I have signed a foolish decree," said the king, "but I cannot call it off. Therefore, you must be tossed to the lions this very night. I know that your God will protect you, however, and even I shall pray for you."

Daniel was then taken and lowered into a dungeon filled with hungry lions.

All that night, King Darius prayed in his chambers, refusing to eat or drink in sorrow for his friend. Then, in the early morning, he rushed to the dungeon and called:

"Daniel, Daniel, are you safe?"

At first, there was only silence from the den of the lions. Again the king cried out: "Daniel, answer me!"

And from the bottom of the dungeon, Daniel replied:

"I am unharmed, O King, for God has protected me, knowing that I am innocent. Last night, He sent an angel from heaven into the dungeon, and, though the lions were fierce and hungry, they made no attempt upon my life. Indeed, they are as gentle as a flock of sheep."

Darius was overjoyed, and he ordered Daniel's immediate release. Then he arrested the wicked Persians who had plotted against his friend. They were thrown to the hungry lions, who devoured them on the spot.

"From this time forth," decreed the king, "all the people of my kingdom shall worship the God of Daniel, for He is the one true God in all the world; and His kingdom will endure forever and ever."

The people accepted this decree, and, when Darius died, the new king, Cyrus, continued to lead a righteous life, with Daniel as the chief of all his ministers.

Daniel's Prophecies

FOR MANY YEARS, Daniel served the kings of Persia as advisor and friend. But he never forgot his own people, the Jews. Over and over, he could hear them praying for the day when they might return to their homeland in the west.

Many years before, Jeremiah had prophesied that, after seventy years, the captives would be freed and allowed to leave Babylon. It was almost that time, and Daniel decided to devote his old age to the task of helping his people return to their homes.

Thus, he prayed and fasted every day, wearing sackcloth instead of his fine garments, and covering his head with ashes as a sign of humility. For many months, Daniel prayed to God in this fashion.

Then, one night, he saw an angel descending from heaven in a halo of light. At first, the prophet was unable to speak, and he fell face down to the ground in fear and wonderment.

But the angel said:

"Do not be afraid, for I have come to help you and reveal many wonderful prophecies of God."

Then the angel took Daniel to the river front, and, in the reflections of the water, he revealed the following things that were to happen to the People of Israel:

First, the Jews would return to their homeland and rebuild the sacred Temple. Then they would become guilty of sinful wickedness once again, and strangers would come and take away their land. After many, many years they would return, under foreign rule, and the Messiah would come into the world to relieve their sins. All these things would happen in the distant future.

When Daniel awoke the next day, he wrote all the angel's words in a book, and he rejoiced in his heart, for he knew that his people would be free. Indeed, King Cyrus soon after sent a proclamation throughout the land, in which he said:

"The Lord has ordered me to rebuild the Temple of Jerusalem. Therefore, I shall free the Jews to return to their homes and undertake this task. I shall also give them all the precious treasures that Nebuchadnezzar took from their Temple. This is as the Lord commands. Therefore, let all those who wish to go assemble at the river."

Over forty thousand Jews eagerly and happily packed their belongings, and prepared for their return to Judah. They were led by a brave young man named Zerubbabel, who was to become the ruler of Jerusalem under King Cyrus' command.

But not all the Jews wanted to return, for some had become very prosperous in Babylon. Instead, they sent money and presents to help those who were heading back. Many other generous people in Babylon gave money and food to the departing Hebrews.

And so the people set out, bravely, to rebuild Jerusalem and the sacred Temple. As for Daniel, he would wait behind and pray. In the words of the Bible: "Happy is he that waiteth . . . for he shall rest at the end of his days."

THE BOOKS OF

EZRA

AND

NEHEMIAH

*The Story of the Rebuilding of the Temple and the Walls
of Jerusalem; and of the Second Covenant with God.*

Rebuilding the Temple of Jerusalem

"TODAY WE SHALL LAY the cornerstone of the Temple," commanded Zerubbabel, "and tomorrow we shall start the foundation here on Mount Zion. Let us work until we have finished our sacred task."

The Jews rejoiced. For years, they had been captives in Babylon. Now they were home at last, and prepared to rebuild not only the Temple but all of Judah, as well. And

so the Jews—young and old—began to clear the rubble and weeds from the ruins of Jerusalem.

To the north of the city lived the idolatrous Samaritans. When they heard that the Jews had returned and intended to rebuild their Temple, they became envious and decided to make trouble. Pretending friendship, they went to Jerusalem and sought out Zerubbabel.

"We are your neighbors from the north," they said, "and we would like to help you rebuild your Temple."

Zerubbabel was suspicious, and informed the Samaritans, in a very polite way, that only the Children of Israel were supposed to work on the sacred building, as ordered by King Cyrus of Persia. The Samaritans were annoyed. They sent presents and bribes to the high officials of Persia along with the following message:

"Do what you can to stop the Jews from rebuilding their Temple."

The wicked Persian officials went to King Cyrus and bothered him every day, urging him to delay the reconstruction. But though the Samaritans interfered with the progress of the sacred work, the Jews nevertheless managed to rebuild at least the foundation of their Temple.

Finally, King Cyrus died, and a man named Artaxerxes came to the throne. He was more receptive to the urgings of the Samaritans, for he believed their evil warnings against the Jews. One day, he ordered all work halted on the sacred Temple. While Artaxerxes lived, only the foundation stood on Mount Zion.

When Artaxerxes died, a second King Darius came to the throne. Like his ancestors and namesake, this new king was generous and understanding. He ordered the Samaritans to leave the Jews alone so that they might complete their sacred work. Unfortunately, the Jews themselves no longer wished to rebuild the Temple.

A prophet named Haggai now appeared in Jerusalem. He climbed upon the foundation of the building and cried:

"You have built yourselves beautiful homes, but the House of God still lies in ruins. Unless you finish this sacred work, all of Judah will be afflicted."

The Books of Ezra and Nehemiah

For years, Haggai preached to the lazy people, and then, at last, when sorrow and affliction came upon Judah, the Jews repented. Immediately, they began to gather wood and stone so that they might complete the reconstruction. To strengthen their cause, King Darius sent a decree threatening severe punishment against anyone who interfered with the important work. Furthermore, the Samaritans, who had caused so much trouble, were ordered to provide food for the priests of Israel so long as the Temple was under construction.

Thus, after many months, the great building was completed, and the people gathered for a solemn celebration. Offerings were made to God, and holy men, such as the prophets Haggai and Zechariah, joined in prayer and song. The Jews were so inspired that they held the feast of Passover for the first time in many years.

Ezra and the King of Persia

WHILE ARTAXERXES was king of Persia and Babylon, a righteous Jew named Ezra lived near the palace. Every day, he heard reports that the Jews who had returned to Judah were having great trouble in keeping the law and the proper worship of God. Ezra had devoted himself to studying the Laws of Moses and felt that he might be able to serve his people in Judah. He therefore asked permission to see the king.

When he arrived before the throne of Artaxerxes, he pleaded for a chance to return to Judah with all those Jews still living in Babylon. The king was sympathetic to his plea and ordered safe conduct for Ezra and his followers. In addition, the king gave the departing Jews many expensive gifts and food.

The courageous Ezra was put in charge of the journey home. He was also responsible for keeping the law. For this reason, he established among the Jews a group of judges who would enforce the commandments of God.

For three days, the Jews prepared for their departure and prayed for guidance. But some of them grew worried in spite of their prayers. They went to Ezra.

"We have no army to protect us in the desert," they said. "It is a long trip to Judah, and there are many bandits and robbers along the way. Let us ask for an army so that we may be safe."

Ezra replied:

"We must trust in God to protect us. If we ask for an army, King Artaxerxes will lose respect for the power of the Lord and His people, and may not allow us to go free."

The people agreed.

Thus, without protection, the Jews began their journey. True to Ezra's words, the Lord safeguarded His people, and, after many months, they arrived in Jerusalem. Ezra was most unhappy with what he found. For one thing, the sturdy walls, which had once protected the city from invaders, were now in ruins. No one had bothered to repair them. Another source of Ezra's unhappiness was the fact that many young people had forgotten God and were marrying out of their religion. Ezra wished to preserve the Jewish faith, and prohibited any marriage to a stranger. After a time, the people came to respect Ezra, and they looked to him for spiritual guidance.

Far away, in Persia, another Jew was turning his eyes toward Jerusalem, in order to help his people. His name was Nehemiah.

Nehemiah and the Walls

AS CUPBEARER to King Artaxerxes, Nehemiah had a very important position in Persia. He was responsible for the king's wine, which meant that he had to be a trustworthy man—if someone tried to poison the king, Nehemiah would know. During the time in which he served Artaxerxes, Nehemiah was very loyal.

One day, bad news reached Nehemiah. The Jews of Jerusalem were having great difficulties in rebuilding the city, and the protective walls that once had encircled Jerusalem were still in ruins. Nehemiah knew that the Jews would be open to an easy attack if their enemies decided to invade. Determined to help his people, he approached King Artaxerxes, and asked permission to enter Jerusalem for the purpose of rebuilding the city's walls.

The king was very fond of Nehemiah, and did not wish him to leave Persia.

"How long do you think this journey will take?" he asked.

And Nehemiah replied,

"About two years. During this time I will need Your Majesty's protection and letters of permission to complete my task. I hope that I may have them."

Artaxerxes was generous and gave Nehemiah permission to rebuild the walls of Jerusalem. He also sent letters to his subjects throughout the kingdom urging them to help the Jews in their task. Gratefully, Nehemiah accepted the king's good wishes, and, with a small group of soldiers, he left Persia.

After many months, Nehemiah arrived at the outskirts of Jerusalem. There he found the walls in ruins, just as he had been told. Sadness filled his heart to see the glory of his people in such destruction; and he became more determined than ever to

fulfill his mission. On the following day, he called all the elders of the city together, and said to them:

"Without strong walls to guard Jerusalem you are weak and open to attack by your enemies. Therefore, let us work swiftly and without stop, as commanded by the king, until every stone is safely in place."

The Jews were enthusiastic. Under Nehemiah's leadership, they set to work immediately. But, as usual, there was trouble. Certain foreigners who lived near Jerusalem were unhappy with the idea of a well-protected city. Others were jealous of Artaxerxes' friendship toward the Jews. These troublemakers made fun of the walls, hoping to discourage the Jews.

"These walls will crumble if a fox walks over them," they said, and laughed. "What a waste of time!"

But the Jews would not be discouraged. Seeing this, their enemies turned to stronger measures, banding together to invade Jerusalem while the walls were still

The Books of Ezra and Nehemiah   *277*

incomplete. But God had spoken to Nehemiah and prepared him for treachery. Thus, when the invaders approached Jerusalem, they found an army of Jews waiting for them. The enemies turned back without trying to attack.

From then on, half the men of Jerusalem repaired the walls while the other half kept guard with spears and swords. For nearly two months, the work went on at a feverish pace. The Jews were nearing completion of their walls, when trouble began all over again, this time among the people themselves. A group of poor men went to Nehemiah, and reported:

"We have worked so long on these walls that our money is running out. Because of this we have had to borrow from our wealthier neighbors. Now they want to be paid or they will take our children as slaves."

Nehemiah was furious. He forced the rich to withdraw their threats and made them swear before the priests of God that they would not take advantage of their poorer brethren. When the foreigners outside the city heard about this trouble, they took heart.

"We will invite Nehemiah to meet with us," they said, "and, when he is outside the city, we will kill him."

And so they sent messages to Nehemiah inviting him to attend a feast that they were giving. But he knew it was a trick, and refused.

The Books of Ezra and Nehemiah

"I have more important work in Jerusalem," he said.

The enemies tried to threaten him.

"We will report you to Artaxerxes," they said. "We will tell him that you are planning to make yourself king of Jerusalem."

"Tell him what you like," Nehemiah replied. "He will know that it is false."

Several times the foreigners tried to lure Nehemiah outside the city, but they always failed. Finally the great walls were complete and the bronze gates inserted. Now Jerusalem would be safe.

To celebrate their success, the Jews held a day-long parade, which started at the walls of the city and continued to the Temple of God. All day, silver trumpets were heard in joyous fanfare, and the people danced in the streets.

Nehemiah was pleased that his task was completed, and he prepared to return to Persia. Before leaving, he established a system of sentries for the wall, so that no enemy could sneak up on the city.

The Second Covenant

NOW EZRA, WHO WAS very old, called all the Jews to the main gate of the wall and there he unfolded a long scroll, which he read to them line by line, without skipping a word. It was the Law of Moses, which had been forgotten for many years. When the people heard God's commandments, they realized how greatly they had sinned, and they wept and repented.

"Let us rededicate ourselves to the Law," said Ezra to the people. "We shall have a second covenant with God, as did Abraham, our father before us. And, to prove our faith, let us each sign a scroll pledging obedience to God and the conduct of a righteous life."

Everyone agreed, and solemnly signed the second covenant. Then Nehemiah departed for Persia, leaving behind him a well-protected city and an upright people.

Some time later, Nehemiah received permission from Artaxerxes to return to Jerusalem. Ezra was dead and the Temple had not been kept holy nor was the Sabbath being properly observed by the people. Nehemiah was sorely grieved at this lack of faith, and he commanded that the Temple be cleansed, and that the proper ceremonies should once again be held there. Then he ordered the gates of the city be shut on the Sabbath so that merchants and traders could not come and go with their wares, and do business in Jerusalem on the holy day. And Nehemiah always strove to keep the children of Israel in the ways of the Lord, and did all he could to keep them from straying.

THE

BOOKS OF

ESTHER, JONAH,

AND JOB

Stories of the Jewish People in Foreign Lands; of Esther,
Who Became a Queen; Of Jonah, Who Was Swallowed by a
Whale; and of Job, Who Kept His Faith in God.

Esther Becomes Queen of Persia

KING AHASUERUS OF PERSIA was mighty, and his palace in the city of Shushan was the center of a gay and exciting life.

Giving large parties was a passion with King Ahasuerus. One party lasted a whole week, and everyone in Shushan—both great and small—was invited. According to custom, the women dined in the palace and the men in the courtyard of the palace garden. Ahasuerus' wife, Queen Vashti, was hostess to the ladies.

Toward the end of the feast, the king became very gay. Holding his goblet in his hand, he called for the queen, and commanded that she appear before him with her crown upon her head. He wished to show his beautiful wife to all the men of Persia.

But Vashti was furious. She did not want to be put on display, and she refused to obey the king's command.

"My wife will not do as I ask," said the angry king. "How shall I punish her?"

"Take away her crown," answered his advisors. "If she is not severely punished, all the women of Persia will think that it is proper to disobey their husbands; and that will be terrible for us."

The king agreed, and proclaimed throughout the land that Vashti was no longer his queen. He also called for a contest among the women of Persia to see which one should fill her place.

"I will seek out the most beautiful maiden in all the land," said the king. "She will become my wife and my queen."

At this same time, there was a Jewish man named Mordecai, who was a gatekeeper at the palace of the king. He heard about Queen Vashti's disgrace and the search for a beautiful maiden. Eagerly he ran home to his cousin, Hadassah. Since her early childhood, Mordecai had raised the dark-eyed girl as though she were his very own daughter. Now he believed that, because of her beauty, God had chosen her to become Ahasuerus' queen.

Hadassah dressed in her finest robes and placed myrtle leaves in her raven hair. Then she prepared to go to the palace for the contest. Before she left home, Mordecai took her aside and said:

"It would be better if you did not reveal that you were Jewish. In fact, we will change your name, for Hadassah is a Hebrew word. From now on you shall be called Esther, which means beautiful. Now go, and God be with you."

Esther took her place in line with the other women who had come for the contest. After a while, King Ahasuerus entered the chamber. He passed from one contestant to the other without showing any interest. But, when he saw Esther, his heart rejoiced. He proclaimed his love for the Hebrew maiden, and in due time she became his queen.

Mordecai Overhears a Plot

WHILE ESTHER LIVED in the palace as Queen of Persia, her cousin Mordecai remained gatekeeper to the king. No one knew that they were related or that Esther was Jewish.

The queen greatly admired her cousin, and often visited him as she strolled in the royal gardens. She relied on him to tell her about the poor people of the kingdom, and about her own kinsmen, the Jews.

One day Mordecai, while at the royal gate, overheard two men plotting against the life of the king. It was their plan to surprise him at a feast and stab him to death. Mordecai immediately sent a message to his cousin with a warning for Ahasuerus.

The laws of Persia were very strange. No one could enter the king's private rooms without his permission. Anyone doing so faced the possibility of death. This law applied to Esther, the queen, as well, and she dared not risk her husband's wrath. So she waited until he passed her chambers, and then she told him of the plot.

"The gatekeeper Mordecai discovered this treachery," she said.

The king was very grateful. He had the traitors arrested and he inscribed Mordecai's name in the royal book of good deeds.

Haman and Mordecai

IN THE PALACE of Ahasuerus were many princes who sought favor with the king. None of these was more cunning and ambitious than Haman. Year after year, Haman made himself humble and did just as the king desired. Then, one day, he found himself promoted to the highest position in the land.

Now the boastful Haman strutted about in his fine robes and jewels, demanding obedience from all. In fact, a law was passed that everyone should bow down to the ground whenever Haman appeared. One man refused to obey—Mordecai the gatekeeper. Every time Haman appeared at the gate, Mordecai rose to his feet while everyone else dropped to his knees.

"How dare you disobey my command?" Haman cried. "Who gives you that right?"

And Mordecai replied:

"I am a Jew; I bow only to God."

From that day on, Haman hated Mordecai and all the Jews. Each time he passed the gate, Mordecai refused to bow. One day, Haman conceived a terrible plan.

Calling together some friends, he broke straws into various lengths and held them in his hand.

"Choose one of these," he said to his friends. "I want to determine the day and the month in which I shall put all the Jews to death."

Thus, by casting lots in this fashion, Haman decided to wipe out the Jewish people on the thirteenth day of the twelfth month, Adar. He then dressed in his finest robes and went before the king. Ahasuerus trusted his chief advisor and was glad to see him.

"I have important news," said Haman to the king. "Living in Persia is a group of wicked people called Jews. They worship their own God and refuse to obey our laws. I say, put them all to death!"

The king was at first unsure. But Haman continued:

"Then, after we have destroyed them, we may take their homes and money and make ourselves rich."

Ahasuerus was greedy, and approved the plan. He gave Haman his royal ring and told him to do as he pleased. The evil minister quickly ran to his scribes, and decreed the mass execution of the Jews for the thirteenth day of Adar.

Copies of this evil decree were sent throughout the land. Mordecai found one of them near the palace gate. When he realized what Haman was planning to do, he tore his clothing in grief and put on sackcloth and ashes. Then he bowed in prayer before the palace gates, hoping that Esther would somehow hear of her people's terrible danger.

The Books of Esther, Jonah, and Job

The very next day, one of Esther's trusted maids came into her chamber and said:

"I have seen Mordecai, the gatekeeper, wearing sackcloth and covered in ashes as a sign of grief. What can be wrong?"

Esther was puzzled and alarmed. She gave her maid fine garments for Mordecai and told her to deliver them. But the maid returned with the garments and said:

"His grief is so great that he could not raise his head."

Esther was very upset. This time, she sent a trusted messenger to Mordecai in order to learn the source of his grief. Modecai handed the messenger a copy of Haman's decree.

"Show this to the queen," he said, "and tell her to plead for the Jews before the king."

When Esther received the news she was overcome with sorrow and fear. She loved her people, but she knew the temper of Ahasuerus. Calling her faithful messenger again, she wrote a letter to Mordecai.

"I have received the evil news," it said, "but I am afraid to appear before the king. You know the law. If I enter his chamber and he does not hold out his golden staff, it means that he is angry and will put me to death. Dare I go before him?"

Mordecai was determined. He sent the following reply:

"You face death in any event, for our enemies are ruthless. They will kill even you, the queen. Therefore, I urge you to go before the king and save your people. God foresaw this moment when he made you Queen of Persia."

Esther was convinced. She told Mordecai to order a fast among all the Jews of Shushan.

"For three days I will fast and pray," said the queen, "and then I will go before my husband, even on pain of death."

For three days, the pious Jews fasted and prayed for their queen. Then, on the fourth day, Esther put on her finest robes and her crown, and she walked through the inner court of the palace into the private chambers of the king.

There was Ahasuerus on his golden throne looking grim and very stern. Esther's heart skipped a beat as she waited for the signal that would mean life or death.

Slowly Ahasuerus raised his eyes. At first, he seemed surprised to see his queen. But she looked so lovely and so brave that he smiled and extended his golden staff as a sign of his pleasure. Greatly relieved, the brave Esther approached the throne.

"I have come to invite my lord to a feast," said the queen, "and I wish your minister Haman also to attend."

The king was delighted and accepted.

"Have you no other requests?" he asked.

And Esther replied:

"I shall ask you a very special favor tomorrow, at my feast, and I hope that Your Majesty will grant my request."

The king promised to give Esther whatever she asked, even if it were half of his kingdom. The beautiful queen left the royal chamber and returned to her rooms.

Esther's Feast

WHEN HAMAN HEARD that he had been invited to dine with the king and queen, he became more boastful than ever. He strutted about and called attention to his fame. But every time he saw Mordecai, his anger returned.

"I shall never be happy," he thought, "until every Jew is dead—especially Mordecai."

At home, Haman complained about Mordecai again. His friends suggested that he ask the king to execute the Jew by hanging him on a special gallows. The evil minister thought this a splendid idea, and ordered a huge gallows built in the palace yard. Then Haman walked to Ahasuerus' private chambers to make his vengeful plea.

That night, the king could not sleep. Instead, he occupied his mind by thumbing through the pages of his royal book on good deeds. While reading, he came upon the account of Mordecai who had saved his life by reporting the assassin's plot.

"This man has never been rewarded," noted the king. "I shall correct that immediately."

At this very moment, Haman entered the room and bowed. He had come to request permission to hang Mordecai on his gallows. But the king spoke first.

"Tell me, Haman," he said, "how should I reward a man who has done me great service?"

The boastful Haman thought to himself, "He refers to me. Whom else could he mean?"

"O great King," Haman exclaimed, "to honor such a man I would seat him on the king's white horse, dress him in the king's robe and crown, and command one of the noble princes to lead him through the city in triumph."

"So be it," said the king. "Take my robes and my crown to the loyal Mordecai; and you, yourself, lead him through the streets as you have described."

Haman was horrified. But he dared not disobey the king. Gathering the royal robes, he went to his hated enemy and carried out the royal decree. Thus, Haman had to lead the resplendent Mordecai through the city streets—Mordecai, the very man whom he wished to hang on the gallows!

Ashamed and bitter, Haman returned to his house and hid. He was so upset that he forgot about Queen Esther's banquet, and had to be reminded by a messenger. Quickly, he dressed and rushed to the palace.

For a time, Ahasuerus, Esther, and Haman ate in silence while the musicians entertained them. Finally, the king leaned over to his wife and tenderly said:

"You wish to make a request of me? Do not be afraid, for I will grant you any favor."

Esther rose from her place and in a quavering voice she exclaimed:

"I am a Jew, and an evil man has sent forth a proclamation ordering all my people killed, including me. I therefore beg you to save us and to punish the villain."

Ahasuerus was amazed.

"Who ordered such an evil decree?" he demanded.

Bravely, Esther pointed to Haman and cried:

"Haman! He is the man!"

The king became furious. He rose to his feet, overturning the banquet table in rage.

"How shall I punish him?" he asked.

"There!" cried one of his guards, pointing to the window. "Someone has built a gallows in the courtyard."

"Excellent," shouted the king. "I order that Haman be hanged there this very morning. Only then will I be satisfied."

That morning, the wicked Haman was hanged on the gallows that he had prepared for Mordecai. But his evil decree to execute the Jews was still in effect, and, according to Persian law, it could not be repealed.

Mordecai went before the king.

"Arm the Jews with swords and spears," he said, "so that they may defend themselves before their enemies. Then let everyone know that we are no longer defenseless and weak. That will save us."

Ahasuerus agreed. When the thirteenth day of the twelfth month dawned, no one in all Persia dared harm the Jews. Instead, a great celebration was held throughout the land, and the people cheered the brave Queen Esther and the wise Mordecai. To this day, the feast of Purim is celebrated in honor of the beautiful Jewish maiden who was the queen and kept her people from being destroyed.

A Fish Swallows Jonah

IN THE PROVINCE of Galilee lived the prophet Jonah. He was a righteous man who often preached about God's eventual judgment. The Lord was pleased with Jonah, and decided to send him on a mission to the great city of Nineveh, in the kingdom of Babylon.

"Arise and go to Nineveh," said the Lord. "The people there have sinned, and I will punish them severely. You must tell them of My anger."

Jonah was surprised. The people of Nineveh were not Jews, he thought. Why should God be concerned with them? Besides, Nineveh was a very wicked city, far from home, and Jonah was unwilling to risk his life just to save some heathens. Therefore, instead of obeying the Lord, Jonah secretly boarded a ship headed in the opposite direction.

When the ship was in the middle of the sea, one day out from shore, a terrible

storm arose. Darkness, thunder, and lightning filled the air, and a great wind fiercely rocked the ship, so that its mast creaked and swayed as though it would break. The sailors and passengers on the ship were terrified. They threw part of their cargo overboard, hoping to lighten the load, but still the boat rocked dangerously in the waters amid great waves.

Finally, the captain of the ship issued a command.

"Let everyone fall to his knees and pray to his gods," he said. "In this way we may be saved—for surely someone on this ship has sinned and offended his god."

Far below, in his cabin, Jonah paid no attention to the storm. Instead, he curled up in his bunk and fell asleep. When the captain learned this, he rushed to Jonah and said:

"Wake up, you sleeper! Pray to your God! Perhaps He can save us from this storm."

After the captain left his room, Jonah began to fear that he was the cause of the storm. His fears were confirmed when he heard the sailors crying:

"Someone has sinned on this ship, and God is punishing him."

To find out who it was, the sailors drew lots among themselves and all the passengers. The shortest lot fell to Jonah, proving his guilt.

"Who are you, and what sin have you committed?" cried the sailors.

Jonah confessed.

"I am a Hebrew," he said, "and I have disobeyed the Lord. If you want to be saved, you must throw me overboard and let me drown."

The sailors did not want to kill Jonah, and tried to outrun the storm. But the harder they tried, the more imperiled they became. Finally, begging forgiveness from God, they threw Jonah over the side of the ship into the dark and dangerous waves.

As soon as the prophet hit the water, the storm subsided and the dark clouds disappeared. The grateful seamen knew that Jonah's God was very powerful; nevertheless, they regretted having drowned the prophet.

But Jonah did not drown. As he sank below the waves, an enormous fish, as big as a house, swallowed him in one gulp. Alone in the dark belly of the fish, Jonah knew that God wished him to live so that he might go to Nineveh and preach. For three days and nights, Jonah crouched within the fish, praying to the Lord for forgiveness.

Jonah in Nineveh

ON THE FOURTH DAY, Jonah felt the fish heaving and tossing in the waters. Then, suddenly, the prophet was cast out of the belly of the fish onto dry land. Looking around, Jonah saw that he was on the outskirts of a large, strange city. He brushed himself off and began walking toward the center of town.

"Where am I?" he asked some passers-by.

"This is Nineveh," they replied.

At last, Jonah realized that he could not escape his mission. With determination in his heart, he set out to preach the word of the Lord in the streets and byways of the city.

"Prepare to meet your God!" he cried. "For the Lord will destroy Nineveh in forty days as punishment for all its sins and wickedness."

When the king of Nineveh heard this warning, he became afraid. Knowing the God of Israel to be powerful and mighty, he sent a decree ordering the people to fast and pray in repentance for their sins. The people of Nineveh, even though they were not Jews, believed in the power of God and truly repented.

For weeks, no one danced or made merry in Nineveh, and the murmurs of prayer could be heard throughout the streets. God was pleased. But the prophet Jonah was annoyed and he said to God:

"I warned these people that in forty days they would be doomed. Now You have forgiven them, and I look like a fool. It would be better if I were dead."

Then, pouting like a little child, Jonah took leave of Nineveh. He walked up into the mountains to a spot overlooking the entire town.

"Perhaps the Lord will change His mind and destroy the city after all," the prophet thought. "I shall wait and see."

Jonah then built himself a small hut and waited. After a time he became very uncomfortable, for it was terribly hot in the sun. Complaining of the heat, Jonah lay down to sleep. When he arose in the morning he found that a luxurious palm tree had grown up right over his shack, providing him with shade. He was grateful, indeed. Still he could not be completely happy, for there was Nineveh stretched out before him, and the Lord had not yet destroyed it.

The next day Jonah awoke in dismay. His luxurious palm tree was all shrunken and dead, for a worm had eaten its roots. Now without shade, Jonah began to suffer in the heat. Before long, hot winds came up out of the east and beat upon his head. He turned red as fire, and was in such agony that again he called on God to strike him dead.

But the Lord replied:

"You are angry because the palm tree wilted and died. But this was not your palm tree; you did not make it. If a dying tree can cause you such sorrow, why have you no mercy on Nineveh? Here is a great city of thousands of people, thousands of cattle, and many buildings. Why should they be destroyed if they repent?"

Tears of pity filled Jonah's eyes. He realized at last that God was merciful to all the people of the earth, and that the salvation of even one man, in a distant city, was worth every effort of the Lord.

Job: The Prologue

ONCE, IN THE LAND OF UZ, there lived a good man named Job. Great wealth and comfort were his, and he had a large and happy family. No one prayed more earnestly than Job. He prayed for his children lest they sin unknowingly, and he was kind to his neighbors, to strangers, to beggars, and to all the poor.

In heaven, God sat upon his lofty throne and the angels clustered at His feet. Among the angels was Satan, the devil, who had crept into the sacred company. With mischief in his heart, he rose to speak before God.

"I have been roaming upon the earth," the devil said. "And I do not think that Man loves God."

The Lord replied,

"There is one man who is righteous above all others. His name is Job. Have you not seen him?"

And the devil laughed.

"Why shouldn't Job be righteous and good? You have given him all manner of wealth and happiness. See what happens if he should lose his livestock and his house and his children. He will surely curse You to Your face."

God knew the heart of Job. He ordered Satan to undo all Job's wealth and happiness.

"We will see if he will curse Me to My face," said the Lord. "Try your evil. But do not lay a hand upon Job to harm him."

Then Satan quickly departed to do his work.

The First Ordeal

NOW GREAT MISFORTUNE fell upon Job. While he was sitting in his house a servant came running breathlessly through the door and shouted,

"Tribesmen from the east have attacked your cattle and carried them off. They have killed our herdsmen—all of them. Only I escaped to tell you."

Job was astonished. Before he could recover from the news, another servant rushed into the house crying,

"Lightning has struck the sheepfold and burned it down. All the sheep are dead, and the shepherds with them. I alone escaped to tell you."

Misfortune followed upon misfortune. In the same afternoon, Job learned that his cattle had been destroyed, his sheep burned, his camels and asses plundered, and all his servants killed. By the time the sun had set, it seemed no greater sorrow could befall the once happy man. But now a servant came running up the path, crying:

"Job, Job! Your children were seated together in the field when a tornado came out of the sky and killed them all in one blow. I alone escaped to tell you."

Job fell to the floor and tore his cloak in grief. But his faith was strong. Instead of crying out against God, he said:

"The Lord has given, and the Lord has taken away. Blessed be the name of the Lord."

The Second Ordeal

WHEN SATAN LEARNED of Job's great faith, he immediately returned to the throne of God. The Lord was pleased with Job and said:

"You have tried to break the faith of My servant Job, but he has remained steadfast."

The devil laughed:

"The misfortunes that befell him did not directly cause him pain. See what will happen if he should become ill and miserable. He will surely curse You to Your face."

The Lord had faith in Job. He instructed the devil to afflict Job with illness and with pain. Satan quickly went about his evil work.

From that day on, Job became desperately ill. His skin broke out in painful boils. The hair fell from his head. His teeth rattled in his jaw. He was so miserable that he placed sackcloth upon his body and sat among the ashes as a sign of grief. His wife came out of the house. She saw her husband's painful condition, and she cried out in despair:

"How can you have faith in God after all this misery? Curse Him, and maybe He will have mercy and let you die."

But Job would not speak against God.

"When the Lord is good to us," he said, "we do not complain. Should we not accept evil when the Lord chooses to send us evil?"

Thus the days dragged on, and Job sat among the ashes in pain and suffering, and his faith began to falter. Then, one day, three of his friends came down the path to visit him and comfort him. They were Eliphaz, Bildad, and Zophar. When they saw Job's miserable condition, they began to weep. So great was their sympathy that they could not even speak. They simply sat silently watching their unhappy friend. Then, at last, Job lifted his eyes and cried out in anguish:

"Perish the day on which I was born, the night when they said, 'The child is a boy.' May that day be blotted out from memory. May it be cursed and forgotten, because mine is a life of meaningless misery. I am greatly afflicted. I sigh and groan. I have no peace, no rest."

When Job's friends heard him speak, they tried to comfort him. This is how it went:

ELIPHAZ: If we try to have a word with you, will you mind? We look at you, once happy and once so good, and we wonder. Have you perhaps lost your faith through sin? Perhaps that is why you are suffering. Think! What innocent person suffers like this? Man himself makes his own mischief, just as sparks fly upward. If I were you, I would appeal to God and try to find out how you have sinned against Him.

JOB: I am overwhelmed with more trouble and pain than there is sand in the sea. Your words are, therefore, no comfort. Can you think of any sin I have done against you or any man? Have I ever been insincere or given to falsehood? You say that I have lost my faith in God. But I have never spoken against Him in all this anguish, for I know that man cannot live forever. What is man that God should pay him any heed?

BILDAD: But it must be that you have sinned, for God does not punish without reason. Repent, and once again the Lord will fill your mouth with laughter and your lips with rejoicing.

JOB: God is wise and mighty in strength. He makes the mountains and He can destroy them. He commands the sun and seals up the stars. Therefore, He must know what He is doing in so afflicting me. Perhaps it is His will to afflict the innocent and reward the guilty. For I am innocent, and I know it. But you do not believe me. Even if I laid aside my sadness in spite of my pains, you would not believe that I am innocent. You would say that I have challenged God.

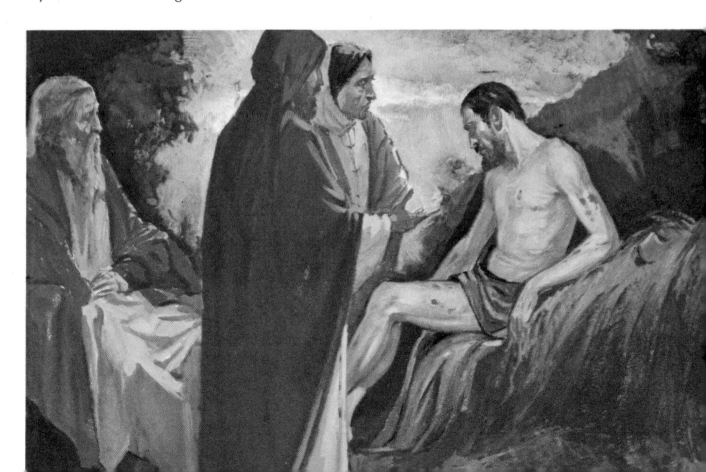

ZOPHAR: And yet you do challenge God by refusing to seek the cause of your punishment. Do this, and you will be freed from your misery. Your pain will wash away like water.

JOB: You offer useless remedies to me, for I am innocent, unless being human is a sin. Man, born of woman, is short-lived and full of trouble. Is any man, therefore, free of sin?

ELIPHAZ: There! You have said it. There *is* some sin upon your soul. Perhaps you have wronged an innocent man. Were you ever unkindly to a beggar? Did you steal unknowingly? Think of all the wicked things that you may have done.

JOB: You do not comfort me. You ask me to think about my sins. Have I not enough to think about? My wealth is gone; my children are dead; and I am wracked with illness. I cannot sleep without the fear of awful dreams. I cannot eat. And yet you come to make it worse for me.

BILDAD: We have spoken as we see fit to speak. If a man is so severely punished, then there must be a reason.

JOB: Why don't you pray for me, instead of all these unkind words? Or if not, leave me. I never asked you to come.

ZOPHAR: Only a wicked man would speak like this to his friends.

ELIPHAZ: Only a sinner who has angered God.

JOB: You talk like this of a man who once was honored and loved throughout the land. A man who once had happy children and a happy home! Don't you see? God has afflicted me for no reason at all. Therefore, I complain. I tear my clothing and I weep. For, in all my life, I never did any man harm, nor was unkind, or cruel. I always worshiped God and loved Him. Why am I punished?

God's Reply

WHEN JOB HAD SAID these words, he closed his eyes and bowed his head. Then another man named Elihu stepped forward. He had been listening to the conversation among Job and his friends, but, being younger than the rest, he felt that it was not proper to speak until they had finished. His words were none the less disturbing to Job. He too accused him of a sin against God. He also criticized the others.

"You have not helped Job," he said. "You point out that he has sinned, but you have not helped him find his sin, so that he might be forgiven. Behold, God is great, and we know Him not."

The friends began to argue among themselves, while Job cried out in pain:

"Why, why, am I so afflicted?"

Then, all at once, a storm brew up out of the heavens, and God spoke to Job with the voice of the wind:

"Is this Job who asks so ignorant a question?" said the Lord. "Has Job lost his faith and courage? You seek many answers to explain your suffering, and you want to know the ways of God. But you do not know how the earth was created, and yet it does exist. You do not know the mysteries of the oceans, and yet the oceans continue to turn and toss. You did not create the stars in the sky, and yet each night they appear and each morning they fade with the sun. You know nothing of man or beast, and yet man lives and moves and breathes. Of all these things you are ignorant, and yet these things exist, for I alone understand My purpose and My plan."

Job then lifted his eyes and answered the Lord most humbly:

"It is true. All these things You can do, and there is a purpose behind Your every deed. Such truth I have always known, but pain and suffering have made me weak. I repent ever doubting the justice of Your deeds. I ask forgiveness and will accept my fate in perfect faith."

The Lord was pleased. He spoke to Eliphaz, and scolded him and the others for being cruel to Job in accusing him of sin.

"I have My reasons for all things," said God. "And man does not always understand them."

Eliphaz and his friends begged Job to pray for them, so that God might forgive ignorance. Job fell on his knees, still aching with pain, and prayed for his erring friends.

Then, slowly but surely, the boils disappeared from Job's body and the pain vanished, and health was restored to the once-suffering man. At the same time, the warm sun shone forth and Job's fields began to flourish with wheat and corn. His flocks increased. Within a year he had more cattle than ever before. And, in due time, seven strong sons and three beautiful daughters were born to him in perfect happiness.

For many, many years Job lived in peace and in comfort such as he had never known. In all of this, he remembered the greatness of God.

"The Lord gives and the Lord takes away," he exclaimed. "Blessed be the name of the Lord."

THE

APOCRYPHA

THE BOOKS
OF TOBIT, JUDITH,
SUSANNA, AND
THE MACCABEES

Stories of Tobit and His Son Tobias, and of Sara, the Unhappy Bride ;
Stories of the Brave Widow Judith, Who Slew General Holofernes ;
Stories of the Righteous Susanna, Who Was Accused
by the Elders in Babylon ; Stories of the Brave Brothers Maccabee,
Who Freed Their People from Bondage.

Tobit and His Son

TOBIT LIVED IN NINEVEH in the days of the captivity. He had been brought from the hills of Galilee in Israel with his wife Anna and their small son Tobias.

For a time, the family led a pleasant life under King Shalmaneser. There was enough food, and the Jewish people were treated fairly. Tobit made it a practice to visit his brethren who were sick, and he was often responsible for seeing that the poor were decently buried when they died.

But evil days fell upon the Jews in Babylon when King Sennacherib came to the throne. He passed a strict law that said: if any Jew died or was killed on the streets, his body was to be dragged outside the city walls and left for the vultures and the wild dogs. Tobit was horrified by this news. Stealthily at night, he crept out of the city and, single-handed, buried the dead according to the Hebrew law. All this he did at the risk of his own safety.

For many years, the cruel Sennacherib ruled in Babylon and Assyria. All this time, Tobit saw to the proper burial of the dead. He was often under suspicion for his deeds, and, eventually, soldiers came to his house and took away his furniture and valued belongings. They also prevented anyone in Nineveh from giving him employment. His wife Anna complained:

"What good have they been, all these righteous deeds in the name of God? You have lost your money, and now we may starve."

Tobit felt sorry for his wife, and promised to stay in the house and avoid trouble. But, one day, his son Tobias rushed up to him and said, "One of our Jewish neighbors has been strangled by the enemy, and his body lies in the street with no one to bury it."

Tobit could not allow such a disgrace, and he left his house and immediately proceeded to bury his neighbor. On returning from his errand of mercy, Tobit realized that he could not enter his house for his hands were still unclean, after the burial. It was late, so he decided to sleep in the garden. In the morning, he awoke with a burning pain in his eyes. During the night some bird lime from a swallow's nest in an overhanging tree had fallen on his face. Now poor Tobit was blind.

He went into his home, where his weeping wife tried to take care of him. In all his suffering, he prayed to God for the strength to continue his charity among the Jews.

The Unhappy Bride

IN THE DISTANT KINGDOM of the Medes, Tobit had a cousin named Raguel. Raguel's daughter Sara lived under a terrible curse, for a demon named Asmodeus was in love with her, and mysteriously murdered every young man who tried to marry Sara. The townspeople could not see Asmodeus, for he was invisible. Therefore, they blamed Sara for the murders, and she had to hide in her room for fear of unjust punishment.

God conceived a plan to help both Tobit and Sara, the daughter of Raguel. He sent the Angel Raphael to earth disguised as an ordinary man. Raphael journeyed to Tobit's home and waited on the road. He knew that his services would soon be needed.

Inside the house, the blind Tobit called Tobias, his son, and said:

"We are poor and without money. But, years ago, I provided for such a time. I left a great quantity of silver in trust with my friend Gabael in the land of the Medes. Now you must journey there and bring back our money, so that you may marry and be prosperous."

Tobias agreed; but he was unsure about the route, and was afraid that he might get lost or even robbed and murdered, far from home. Tobit decided to hire a guide for his son, and instructed Tobias to seek an honest man who knew the route to Media.

At the same moment, there was a knock on the door. Outside stood Raphael, the angel, who had come to offer his services as a guide. Tobit was satisfied with the stranger's qualifications and agreed to hire him.

"What is your name?" Tobit asked.

And Raphael replied:

"I am Azarias, and we are distantly related, you and I."

"Go then, Azarias," said Tobit. "Take my son to the land of the Medes and see that no harm comes to him. When you return I will pay you well."

Then Tobit blessed his son and sent him off with Azarias. Anna wept to see her son go off on such a long journey, and Tobias' little dog also whimpered and scratch-

ed at the door until he was freed to follow his master.

When they had traveled several miles, Tobias and Azarias decided to rest by the banks of a river. While Azarias prepared a fire, Tobias laid aside his clothes and jumped into the water in order to bathe.

Suddenly, a strange fish came swimming toward Tobias with its fearsome jaws opened wide.

"Help me, Azarias," called the young man. "A fish has attacked me!"

Azarias ran to the shore and cried:

"Grab the fish by his fins, and he will become helpless."

Tobias obeyed. In a flash, the fish became limp and helpless. With the catch in hand, Tobias dashed out of the water and huddled near the fire that Azarias had kindled.

"This fish will be good to eat," the angel said. "But, first, you Tobias, must cut it open and remove its heart, liver, and gall. Wrap these in cloth and put them in your pocket. Who knows? These may be useful, some day."

Tobias followed Azarias' instructions. He opened the fish, removed the heart, liver, and gall. Then he and his guide ate the fish.

In the morning, Tobias, the angel, and the little dog joyfully continued their journey toward Media. As they walked, Tobias questioned his friend.

"Of what importance are the heart, the liver, and the gall of the fish?" he asked. And Azarias answered:

"The heart and liver, put on burning coals, will drive away demons, for they are afraid of the smell. The gall is an excellent cure for certain kinds of blindness. All these things we shall learn of presently."

The Books of Tobit, Judith, Susanna, and the Maccabees

By midday, the two were in Media, and went directly to the home of Raguel, Tobit's cousin. Before they entered the house, Azarias took Tobias aside and said:

"Raguel has a lovely daughter who is most unhappy. She will make an excellent bride for you, and I shall speak to her father on your behalf."

Tobias was, at first, delighted. But then he remembered the stories that he had heard about Sara of the land of the Medes.

"Is she not the girl who is supposed to have murdered seven husbands?" questioned Tobias in alarm.

The angel smiled, and assured Tobias that all would be well, if he kept faith in God.

Tobias Marries Sara

IN DUE TIME, the wedding between Sara and Tobias was arranged. Raguel approached the day with mixed emotions. On the the one hand, he was happy to see his daughter engaged to such a fine young man. On the other, he believed that Tobias would die on his wedding night, like all the others. Sara, too, was unhappy. She loved Tobias but feared for him, for the evil Asmodeus had sworn to kill every husband whom Sara brought into her house.

On the night of the wedding, Azarias took Tobias aside and said:

"When you and your bride are alone in the bedroom, take the heart and the liver of the fish. Place these on the fire. The smoke will frighten the demon Asmodeus away, and he will never return. Then you will live happily ever after with your bride."

Tobias did just as he was told, and, that night, while Sara was preparing for bed, he threw the heart and the liver into the flames. In a moment the demon Asmodeus appeared.

"What have you done?" he exclaimed. "I cannot stand that smoke! Take it away!"

But Tobias would not take it away. The smoke grew very thick and filled the room with a terrible stench that caused Asmodeus to choke and cough until he could stand it no more—and, in a flash, he disappeared, never to be seen again.

In the morning, Raguel waited fearfully at the door of the bedroom, for he thought surely Tobias was dead. But to his delight, when the door opened, there stood bride and bridegroom in perfect happiness.

"We will hold a great feast!" cried Raguel.

Tobias then sent servants to Gabael, his father's friend, with an invitation to the feast. At the same time, Gabael was to bring the silver that he had kept for Tobit so many years.

The celebration for Tobias and Sara lasted fourteen days. Raguel was so happy for his daughter that he would not permit the feast to end. Every time the food and drink ran low, he cheerfully ordered new supplies. But he finally blessed the couple and allowed them to depart.

Tobias Returns Home

BACK IN NINEVEH, Tobit and his wife Anna did not know what had happened, and they feared that their son Tobias was dead. Poor, blind Tobit lost all will to live. One day, when their hope was almost exhausted, the old people heard footsteps on the path. There, at last, were Tobias and Azarias his guide. They were both running toward the house.

Tobit rose from his chair and groped his way to the door, stumbling in his blindness. At that same moment, Tobias entered. Leading his father back to the chair, Tobias withdrew the gall of the magic fish. Carefully he applied the juice of the gall to his father's eyes, just as Azarias had told him. A moment later, the old man cried out in joy:

"I can see! I can see! Praise be the Lord!"

Happiness followed upon happiness. Tobias now told his parents of Sara, his bride, who even at that moment was ap-

proaching in her caravan. The dutiful son also produced the great quantity of silver that he had received from Gabael in Media. So great was Tobit and Anna's joy that they ordered a feast and celebration that lasted for seven days.

When the feast had ended, Tobit called his son to him and said:

"We must now pay Azarias his wages as we promised, so that he may go about his business."

Tobias agreed. He had become very fond of Azarias, and asked his father to reward him with half the quantity of silver that Tobias had brought from Media. Tobit was pleased to do so and called Azarias to his side.

"I am so happy with your services," Tobit said, "that I wish to reward you many times over. You have protected my son, brought him a good wife, and, through your wisdom, helped cure my blindness. Please take this silver with my thanks."

But Azarias would not take the silver; instead he drew Tobit and Tobias aside and declared in ringing tones:

"Behold! I am Raphael, one of the seven holy angels who stand before the throne of God. Tobit has served the Lord, and the Lord is pleased. Therefore, I came here to help you and bring you peace. Your goodness is the only reward that I need."

When the others heard this they fell on their knees, and buried their faces, for the room suddenly became filled with glorious light. In that same instant, Raphael unfolded his wings and departed to heaven. Tobit lifted his eyes:

"Praise be to God," he said. "He has brought us wonderful works and we will bless Him for ever and ever."

The Books of Tobit, Judith, Susanua, and the Maccabees

Holofernes,
the Fierce General

AFTER THE JEWS RETURNED to Jerusalem from the Babylonian captivity, there was trouble in the eastern world. The king of Assyria, offended by the ambassadors of certain smaller countries, decided to teach them a severe lesson. For this purpose, he called upon Holofernes, the fiercest general of his armies.

"Lead your troops against our enemies," said the king. "If they surrender and join you, let them live. If they resist, spare no one, neither man, woman, nor child."

Holofernes was pleased with this order. He loved war and enjoyed the prospects of victory. In the months that followed, he led the powerful Assyrian army in triumph over the smaller countries of the Middle East. Finally, he faced Judah, and the city of Jerusalem.

"Tell the Jews to surrender," he ordered his men. "Tell them to march out of their cities and bow down to me and to my king, or we will kill them all."

The messengers soon returned. They reported that the Jews refused to surrender and were in deep prayer to their God for protection and deliverance. Holofernes was surprised. Never before had he come upon a nation that dared oppose his army and his strength.

"Who are these people?" he asked.

A man named Achior stepped forward to answer the general.

"These are the same people whom Moses led out of Egypt," said Achior. "Many miracles took place in those times, for these Jews have a very powerful God. When they are righteous and pure, their God is kind to them, and gives them victory. When they sin, He turns His wrath against them. Now they are in prayer and they are fasting. Surely their God will help them and grant them victory even over your great strength."

When the soldiers heard Achior they grew afraid and there was much dissension in the ranks. Furiously, Holofernes turned on Achior and accused him of being a Jewish spy, who had come purposely spreading alarming and unreliable stories. As a punishment, he had Achior bound with rope and led back into the hills of Judah.

"Tell your friends that we mean to destroy them all, every man, woman, and child!" said the general.

Achior was tied to a tree on a hillside near the city of Bethulia, and left there by the Assyrians. He was found and released by some Jewish soldiers who took him into the city.

"The fierce general Holofernes is about to attack your city," he announced. "And he will kill me and everyone else whom he finds!"

The people of Bethulia became panicky. From their fortress, they could see Holofernes' enormous army. They could also see the general's tent, surrounded, as it always was, by an armed guard of a hundred men.

"Surely they will defeat us," said the Jews. "Either they will hurl their armies against us or they will starve us out. It would be best for us to surrender."

And so they decided to surrender in five days, unless God came to rescue them.

The Widow Judith

In bethulia there lived a widow, Judith, the most God-fearing woman in the entire city. For three years she had lived in mourning for her husband, who died while working in the fields. Now she heard of the plan to surrender, and she came before the elders of the city.

"You are tempting God," she told them, "by saying that you will surrender in five days unless He rescues us. Have you no greater faith? Perhaps God chooses to help us on the sixth day, or on the tenth. We must pray for our own deliverance."

Then she told the elders that she had a secret plan to defeat the enemy. She asked permission to leave the city that night with her maid.

The elders were impressed with Judith's speech, and agreed to her wish. But they wondered what she, an ordinary woman, could do to save the nation.

Judith returned home, and spent the rest of the day in prayer. Then she removed her widow's weeds and dressed in her most beautiful garments. Upon her head she set a jeweled crown, and upon her arms she placed many bracelets and beads. After this, she called her servant and prepared a large sack of food, for she would not eat anything forbidden by her religion. When she was fully prepared, she walked to the city gates. The elders were amazed to see her beauty, and, though they still did not know what she planned to do, they wished her well, opened the gates, and allowed her to leave.

Judith and her servant roamed the countryside near the Assyrian camp. In the darkness, they could see campfires and the tents of Holofernes' army. As they watched from a clump of trees, a group of soldiers came up behind them.

"What are you doing here?" they demanded.

Judith explained that she and her servant had deserted the Jewish city since they knew that Holofernes would be victorious. Now, Judith continued, she wanted only to serve the great Assyrian general. The soldiers were impressed with Judith's beauty and charm, and they decided to bring her to their general.

There, in his tent, Holofernes was resting beneath a luxurious canopy. When Judith saw him she fell on her knees.

"O great Holofernes," she said, "I am your servant. I have left my people because they are weak, and I know that they will be defeated by your army."

Holofernes was impressed with the beautiful woman and urged her to rise.

Judith continued:

"I am a righteous woman and favored by God. If I pray to Him, He will tell me when the Jews have sinned and when He will abandon them. Then you may attack and easily win."

Holofernes remembered that Achior had told him that God would abandon the Jews if they were wicked. Thus, he believed Judith. From that moment on, he declared, she was to come and go as she pleased within the Assyrian camp.

For three days, Judith prayed silently to God. On the fourth day, Holofernes invited her to a feast in his tent. She accepted, but asked permission to bring her own special food. Holofernes agreed.

When Judith arrived in the general's tent she looked more beautiful than ever

before. As she ate, Holofernes admired her.

"Drink now, and be merry with us," he said. He was sure he had nothing to fear from Judith.

"I will drink gladly," the Hebrew woman replied.

For hours Holofernes ate and drank, all the while boasting of his coming victory over the Jews. By the end of the evening, he was so drunk he fell down fast asleep on his couch.

This was the moment that Judith had awaited. Stealthily, she lifted the general's heavy sword from its place, and, with two mighty strokes, cut off his head at the neck. She then put the head in the bag that had carried her food, and quietly, with her servant, left the Assyrian camp undisturbed and hurried toward Judah.

When Judith arrived at Bethulia the elders were surprised to see her alive. But she had no time to explain, and she urged them to call all the people into the streets. When everyone had assembled, Judith mounted the stairs and withdrew the severed head of Holofernes. Holding it aloft she cried:

"God has delivered us from our enemy because we kept our faith in Him!"

The people shouted for joy and grew bold in their hearts. The Assyrians, meanwhile, having found the headless body of their general, were in complete confusion. It was, therefore, easy for the Jews to defeat them and drive them away. When the battle was won, a great celebration was held throughout the land. The hero of the day was the beautiful widow Judith, who had so bravely slain the fierce Assyrian general.

The Books of Tobit, Judith, Susanna, and the Maccabees

Susanna and the Elders

IN BABYLON, ONE DAY, a man named Joiakim came to the prophet Daniel with a painful story. Joiakim's wife, Susanna, had been accused of unfaithfulness by two respected elders of the city. Now, the court had condemned her to death without listening to what she had to say. Daniel was angered by so high-handed a procedure, and went to hear Susanna's story from her own lips.

"For many days," she told him, "two of the city's elders came to my husband's house to discuss business. I noticed that they often watched me as I walked in the garden with my maids. I felt uncomfortable whenever I saw them, but said nothing.

"It was very hot a few days ago, and I decided to bathe in my garden. I told my maids to lock all the garden gates, so that I would not be disturbed. They set a basin of water before me and brought me many fine oils and soap. Then, because they had other work to do, they left me and returned to the house. When I was alone in my bath, I suddenly saw the two elders, who had come out of hiding. They declared their love for me, and when I shrank from them, they said:

" 'You can't avoid us. If you try, we will say that you have been meeting in secret with a young man here in the garden. Since there are two of us, we shall be believed and you will be condemned as an unfaithful wife.'

"I was afraid, but had faith in God, so I told them not to touch me, and I screamed for help. My maids came running back. The elders immediately accused me of unfaithfulness. They said that I had been entertaining a young man who had broken away from them and left by the garden gate. I was taken to prison—though I am innocent—and now I have been condemned to die."

Daniel heard the story with much compassion, and was convinced of Susanna's innocence.

Filled with indignation, he went to the court where Susanna had been tried, and demanded the right to question the elders. Since he was highly respected, the judges agreed. Daniel then took one of the elders aside, so that the other could not hear. Only the judges were present as Daniel said:

"You testified that Susanna met a young man in her garden and sat with him beneath a large tree. Tell me, what kind of tree was it?"

And the elder replied:

"It was a gum tree."

Daniel then called the other elder before the judges.

"Tell us," he said, "under what kind of tree did Susanna sit with the young man?"

And the second elder replied:

"It was a holly tree."

Then Daniel turned to the entire court and exclaimed:

"These men have lied! This one says it was a holly tree, the other, a gum tree. They made up the entire story because they tried to dishonor Susanna and she would have no part of them. Therefore, let them be punished severely, and let Susanna reclaim the respect and dignity that she rightly deserves."

The court agreed. The elders were put to death, and Susanna and Joiakim were happily reunited.

The Story of the Maccabees

THE HISTORY OF the ancient world is full of war and conquest. One great empire conquered another, enslaving thousands and sending great armies into the field. Egypt was the first of these conquering empires. For a long time, Egyptian power was unchallenged. Then the Assyrians and Babylonians conquered Egypt, and took over all its territories. Israel under Solomon had a brief period of imperial glory—soon ended by Assyria under King Nebuchadnezzar. During the time of the prophet Daniel, the Persians and the Medes conquered Assyria. Under such kings as Darius and Cyrus, the Persian Empire covered most of the known world. From 333 to 327 B.C., Alexander the Great of Greece conquered the Persian Empire and all its holdings. Judah, also called Judea, was part of Alexander's vast empire.

Under Greek rule, the Jews fared well. They were free to worship God and follow the Laws of Moses. Unfortunately, Alexander the Great died when he was very young. There followed great turmoil in the world. Civil wars broke out and various families took control of Alexander's far-reaching empire. First, the Ptolemies ruled Judah. They were followed by the Seleucids, a cruel family of kings who persecuted the Jews and caused much hardship and grief.

Antiochus was a Seleucid king who seemed to take pleasure in persecuting the Jews. First he desecrated the Temple in Jerusalem. All the precious treasures were removed and the holy objects smashed and defiled. Then he ordered severe punishment and death to all those who continued to obey the Laws of Moses. The Jews were once again a broken and sorrowful people. Their sanctuary was laid waste; their feasts were turned into mourning; their Sabbaths were dishonored. They were forced to witness sacrifices made to idols, and all manner of uncleanliness and profanation was put upon them.

As this persecution continued, the Jews grew stronger in their faith. Many went to their deaths rather than eat forbidden food or break the Holy Laws. One family of seven sons suffered the cruelest tortures because they would not eat pork, which the Jews considered unclean. While their aged mother looked on, each of the seven sons was put to death in hideous fashion. But their bravery became a legend, for each son grew more defiant as he saw his brother die. And the aged mother was bravest of all.

"Do not break the faith!" she cried to her sons. She preferred to see them die as Jews and patriots rather than bend to the will of the evil Antiochus. For this, she too was put to death.

In all this suffering and persecution, the Jews did not weaken. Instead, they began to form secret groups of resistance.

One such group was headed by the High Priest Mattathias, who had five sons. Antiochus was wary of Mattathias, who was rich and very influential. One day, the king ordered the priest to renounce his Jewish faith publicly. Mattathias gathered his family and faithful followers and escaped to the hills in northern Judea.

"We will resist the evil tyrant and reclaim our country," announced Mattathias, "even if we must live like beasts in the hills."

Indeed, Mattathias and his sons and their followers did live like beasts in the hills, eating what they could find, while they prepared to attack the enemy.

To lead the Jewish army, Mattathias chose Judas, one of his sons. Because of his great strength and courage, Judas was called Maccabeus or "the hammerer." Soon the entire army became known as the Maccabees.

At first, Judas and his men suffered defeat at the hands of Antiochus. With each setback the Jews retreated to the hills, where they hid and regrouped their forces. Antiochus was not familiar with the hills of Judea and dared not venture out of his cities. For a long time, the rebels were silent, and the tyrant thought that he had conquered them. But Judas and his brothers were gathering new strength.

"We will fast and pray," said Judas to his men. "Then upon my signal, we will strike at the cities of Antiochus and reclaim Jerusalem."

Judas was a brilliant commander. With only six thousand men, he attacked several well-fortified cities and defeated the enemy troops. Then he prepared to invade Jerusalem, the stronghold of Antiochus. For days before the battle, Judas prayed and sacrificed to God in the company of his followers.

Meanwhile, the king, having seen the might of the Maccabees, became afraid and sick with worry. He gathered many of the treasures that he had taken from the Jews and fled the city. But guilt and illness weighed him down. Surrounded by the sacred treasures he had stolen, Antiochus died in agony. He was succeeded by his very young son. This child was no match for the Maccabees. After nearly two hundred years of persecution and enslavement by their enemies, the Jews finally triumphed. Judas led his men into Jerusalem and freed the city.

In order to celebrate their victory, a solemn rededication of the holy Temple was held. For eight days, the grateful people offered sacrifice and homage to God for their deliverance. This great holiday was called the Rededication, or "Chanukah"; and it is celebrated today by the Jews as a remembrance of the brave Maccabees.

For nearly a hundred years thereafter, the Jews were independent and free of foreign rule. Judas became leader of the nation. In due time, he was followed by his brothers and their descendants. But to the west another great empire was forming under a man named Julius Caesar. This was the great Roman Empire that conquered almost the entire world. By the year 66 B.C, Rome had conquered Judea as well, and set

The Books of Tobit, Judith, Susanna, and the Maccabees

up a new family of kings of whom the first was Herod Antipater. These kings were not Jews, but descendants of Esau, and they took their orders from Rome. For centuries thereafter, the Jewish people were under foreign rule or lived dispersed in many parts of the world.

In 1948, during our own times, the State of Israel was proclaimed on the site of ancient Canaan. Once again, the Jews returned to their homeland after great hardship and persecution. Once again, they faced hostility from their neighbors in the Middle East. But, in the spirit of rededication, they rebuilt Jerusalem and the other cities of the Holy Land. Thus, after thousands of years, the Covenant of God with Abraham was fulfilled in the Lord's own words:

> I will establish My covenant between Me and thee and thy seed after thee in their generations, for an everlasting covenant, to be a God unto thee and to thy seed after thee. And I will give unto thee, and to thy seed after thee, the land wherein thou art a stranger, all the land of Canaan, for an everlasting possession; and I will be their God.

The Books of Tobit, Judith, Susanna, and the Maccabees

THE
NEW TESTAMENT

THE NEW

TESTAMENT

THE GOSPELS
OF MATTHEW, MARK,
LUKE, AND JOHN

*Stories of Jesus, Called Christ. The Events in Judea in the
Time of Herod the Great; the Birth of Jesus; His Life;
His Miracles; the Parables He Told; His Death and
Resurrection.*

The Jewish People and Rome

DURING THE DAYS of the Roman Empire, the country of the Jews was known as Judea. A family of kings named Herod ruled over the land, but above them was a Roman governor with a Roman army to enforce his will. The Emperor of Rome allowed Herod to hold court and live in a beautiful palace, but the Roman governor actually passed the laws and carried them out.

The Jews of those days worshiped in synagogues, which were small buildings combining religious study and prayer. Since their great Temple was again in ruins, the synagogues were the only places in which they could congregate to recall the days of their greatness and the deeds of their forefathers.

In their synagogues, the Jews discussed their hope of a Messiah, a Saviour who would come from God to relieve the sufferings and injustices of the world. They had read about this Messiah in the prophecies of Isaiah and Daniel, and it seemed to many that the time was at hand for such a Redeemer to appear.

Of course, there were various groups who had various ideas of how this Messiah

would look and what would happen when he arrived. The Pharisees were a group of Jews who strictly followed the Torah, the Books of Moses, to the last letter. They were studious men, and their teachings were rigid. The Sadducees were another group, many of them well-to-do, who adapted themselves to a more political way of life, and readily accepted the Roman rule. The Pharisees and the Sadducees often quarreled, and accomplished little as a result. Besides these two parties, other groups formed. Some were pious and secluded. Others wandered from town to town preaching, like the early prophets. By and large, few Jewish people belonged to any of these groups. They only yearned for the day when the Messiah, the Redeemer as they called him, would miraculously free them from oppression and ease their suffering.

Herod, though a partly foreign king, tried to gain respect from the Jews by rebuilding their holy Temple. With permission from Rome, he created a splendid building of white stone covered with silver and gold. Many Jews thought this Temple too elaborate and unlike the original Temple of Solomon. For that reason, they preferred to worship in their simple synagogues.

Some accepted Herod's building with open arms. These men were close to the king, and sought his favor. He, in turn, made them priests of the Temple, and dressed them in beautiful robes. Many of these priests became very rich and powerful.

But, even with the Temple, most Jews had little comfort. They were forced to work at simple jobs that earned them little money. On top of this, they had to pay taxes to Rome, to Herod, and to the priests. It was small wonder that poverty existed in the land, and that misery afflicted family upon family in Judea.

Zacharias was the head of a family of priests. Nevertheless, he was poor and humble. With his wife, Elisabeth, he lived quietly in Jerusalem, performing the duties of his religion in a righteous way. Though Zacharias and his wife were well past their youth, they had no children. Every time the good man went to the Temple, he prayed for a son. The years went by, but no child was born. Even so, Elisabeth and Zacharias served God with great devotion.

Then, one day, when he was alone preparing the altar in the Temple, Zacharias saw an angel of God. Fearful and bewildered, the humble priest fell to the floor, and buried his face in his hands. But the angel spoke reassuringly.

"Do not fear me," he said. "God has heard your prayers for a son and will grant your plea. In due time, a boy will be born to your wife Elisabeth. You shall call him John, and he will be filled with the Spirit of God, like the prophets of old."

Zacharias was dumfounded. How could he, a man so old, and his wife, also well past her youth, have a son?

"Please give me proof of your prophecy," he asked the angel.

"I am Gabriel, one of the angels of God," replied the visitor. "And I regret that you ask me for proof. Because of your doubt, you will not be able to utter a single word until the birth of your son. Then you will know that I have spoken the truth."

The angel disappeared, leaving the bewildered priest alone in the Temple. After a while, some people came to inquire why he tarried. When he tried to answer, he found that he could not speak. The angel's prediction had come true.

The Annunciation

ONE DAY in spring, the Angel Gabriel appeared in the city of Nazareth, in the hills of Galilee. There lived the maiden Mary, who was betrothed to marry Joseph, the carpenter.

It was a peaceful day. Mary was seated quietly in her house, reading her prayers.

"Hail," the angel said to her. "The Lord is with thee; among all women art thou most blessed."

Mary humbly lowered her eyes, for she did not understand. Then Gabriel prophesied that Mary would soon give birth to a son—the Hope of the World—and that this son would be called Joshua, or, as we know him, Jesus.

"He shall be great," said the angel, "and he shall be called the Son of the Highest;

and the Lord God shall give unto him the throne of his father, King David. And he shall reign for ever and ever, and unto his kingdom there shall be no end."

Mary bowed her head and replied:

"Whatever the Lord God commands, I will gladly do."

Then Gabriel disappeared, and Mary remained at her prayers in the quiet of her room.

The Visitation

ELISABETH, THE WIFE of Zacharias, was Mary's cousin. She sent word to the younger woman that, by a miracle of God, she was expecting a son. Mary had been told by Gabriel that Elisabeth would so conceive, and she was overjoyed.

Filled with the Spirit of God, Mary journeyed to her cousin's home for a visit. When Elisabeth saw her, she was stirred by Mary's beauty and serenity, and she said:

The Gospels of Matthew, Mark, Luke, and John

"Surely you are blessed among all women and blessed is the fruit of your womb."

Mary lifted her voice in thanks to God for her great fortune.

"My soul magnifies the Lord," she said, "for He has blessed me. And though I be humble, all generations from this time forth will call me blessed, for there is no single thing that the Lord cannot do."

Mary stayed with her cousin Elisabeth for three months, and the two women often talked of the wonders of God and His blessings upon the Children of Israel.

Then Mary returned to Nazareth·and wed Joseph the carpenter. Though he was a humble man in a humble trade, Joseph was descended from the royal house of King

David. He too was visited by an angel in a dream and was told of the wonderful child that Mary was to bear. Being a pious Jew, Joseph was overjoyed to know that the prophecy of Isaiah would be fulfilled, for it said that a Saviour would be born to the family of the House of David in the city of David and that the birth would be like no other in all the world.

The Advent of John

NOW ELISABETH was about to give birth. Many friends and relatives gathered in the house of Zacharias to celebrate the great event.

"What will they name the child?" the neighbors wondered.

"Zacharias, of course," one man said. "It is the custom to name firstborn sons after their fathers."

But Elisabeth interrupted, and announced:

"My husband wished the boy to bear another name that an angel told him long ago. But, since he has lost his speech, we do not know what that name will be."

Zacharias was listening. He beckoned the guests to his side and then with his pen he wrote the name *John* on his writing table. And, in the same instance, his speech returned.

"John shall be his name," said the father joyously.

The people of Judea heard with wonder about the birth, and said, "What manner of child will this be?" For they knew the hand of the Lord was upon him.

And filled with the Spirit of God, Zacharias prophesied:

"Blessed be the Lord God of Israel, for He has visited and redeemed His people. He has raised up a horn of salvation for us in the house of His servant David; as He promised by the mouth of His holy prophets from of old that we should be saved from our enemies, and from the hand of all who hate us, to perform the mercy promised to our fathers and to remember His holy covenant: the oath which He swore to our Father Abraham to grant to us, that, being delivered out of the hand of our enemies, we may serve Him without fear in holiness and righteousness all the days of our life.

"And you, child, will be called the prophet of the Highest; for you will go before the face of the Lord to prepare His ways, to give knowledge of salvation to His people by the remission of their sins, through the tender mercy of our God, whereby the dayspring from on high has visited us, to give light to those who sit in darkness and in the shadow of death, to guide our feet into the way of peace."

And the child grew, and became strong in spirit, and was in the deserts till the day of his appearance to Israel.

The Birth of Jesus

THE PROPHECY of the angel Gabriel was about to be fulfilled, for Mary was soon to bear her son, the infant Jesus. At this same time, a decree went out from Caesar Augustus, the Emperor of Rome, that each man in Judea was to return to the city of his birth so that a census might be taken.

Joseph the carpenter had been born in Bethlehem, a small city some distance from the town of Nazareth, where he and Mary lived. Obedient to the emperor's decree,

Joseph gently placed Mary on a donkey and began the long journey to his childhood home.

When they reached Bethlehem, they found the city crowded and bustling with people, all of whom had come in answer to the emperor's decree. Joseph was concerned, for Mary was close to the time of her delivery, and he went from place to place, seeking shelter. But there was no room for them in the public places.

At one inn the owner told Joseph:

"You may stay in the stable tonight."

So Joseph led his wife into the stable among the horses, the sheep, and all the other gentle creatures. There she gave birth to her son and wrapped him in swaddling clothes and—lacking a cradle—she laid him in a feeding trough, called a manger. Thus was Jesus born.

Not far away, in the peaceful hills, certain shepherds were tending their flocks, when suddenly they saw a glowing angel appear.

"Fear not," he called to them, "for behold, I bring you good tidings of great joy, which shall be to all people. For unto you is born this day in the city of David, which is Bethlehem, a Saviour: Christ the Lord. And this shall be a sign unto you; you shall find the baby wrapped in swaddling clothes, and lying in a manger."

The shepherds rejoiced. At last the long awaited prophecy was at hand and, as they rushed toward Bethlehem to see the newborn child, a brilliant new star shone in the deep black night, and a multitude of heavenly voices exclaimed:

"Glory to God in the highest and on earth peace, good will toward all men."

The Gospels of Matthew, Mark, Luke, and Johu

The Christ Child Is Adored

LIKE A BEACON, steady and bright, the star of Bethlehem pointed the way to the stable where Mary and the baby were sleeping. Joseph watched over them in the light of a little fire he had kindled. How beautiful was the child and how peaceful was the night!

"Let us now go even unto Bethlehem and see this thing which has come to pass," said the shepherds.

Then, outside, quietly and reverently, the shepherds approached the barn; and saw the infant resting in the manger as the angel had described him. Kneeling, they prayed to God and gave thanks for the hope that was now in their hearts. This was the world's first Christmas.

For some time after, Mary and Joseph stayed in the stable caring for the newborn child. Then, after Jesus was circumcised, they journeyed to Jerusalem, so that the baby Jesus might be presented in the Temple. It was the custom in those days for a firstborn Jewish son to be blessed by the priests while his father made the proper sacrifices to God. Joseph obeyed this law, and offered a pair of turtledoves, or pigeons, upon the sacred altar.

While Joseph and Mary were thus in the Temple with their son, an old man named Simeon was praying off in a corner of the building. Every day, he came to pray for the Messiah, believing that he would not

The Gospels of Matthew, Mark, Luke, and John

die until he had beheld the Saviour of the world. Now, as Simeon prayed, he lifted his head and saw Mary carrying Jesus from the altar. Immediately he knew that this was the Holy Child, and he approached Mary and said:

"This child is to be our Saviour. I know it in my heart. Therefore, I pray, let me hold him for a moment, so that I may depart in peace knowing my salvation."

Mary was very kind. She placed her baby in the old man's arms. An aged widow, Anna, also fondled the child, and the two elderly people had tears of happiness in their eyes.

All the while, Mary was somewhat puzzled. She remembered the angel Gabriel and the wonderful things he had said about her child. Yet she wondered; how would this little baby be the Saviour of the world? Did God intend the Messiah to be like everyone else, to be born like a man, to grow up and go to school and to do all the things that other men do? Mary could not answer. Taking her child from Simeon, she returned with Joseph to Bethlehem.

The Visit of the Wise Men

FAR TO THE EAST of Judea, there lived certain wise men called Magi. These wise men (according to tradition, there were three), looked up into the heavens and saw a brilliant, new star. They knew this star represented the birth of the new king of the Jews, and they decided to pay him homage.

So they gathered up many fine gifts and treasures and set out for Judea. All the while, they followed the brilliant star. But, when they came to the gates of Jerusalem, they could not be sure if the star pointed in that direction or just slightly beyond.

"We will ask King Herod," they said.

Herod had not heard about the newborn child. When the noble wise men came before him they asked:

"Where may we find the new king of Israel, so that we may pay him homage?"

The wise men referred to Jesus as a king, not in the sense of one who sits upon an earthly throne, but as a king of goodness and peace. Herod did not understand this. He became immediately fearful that some child had been born who would one day take away his power. But he did not show his fear. Craftily, he said to the wise men:

"The prophets have written that this child would be born in Bethlehem, which is very near. Go there and find that child; then send word where he is, so that I may follow and pay my respects."

Herod had no intentions of paying his respects to the newborn king. In fact, it was his plan to murder Jesus as soon as he found where he lived.

The wise men did not suspect Herod of such an evil plan, and departed toward Bethlehem. Above them, the star shone brightly, ever leading the way to the spot where Mary and Joseph watched over the baby.

"Here at last is the place," said the wise men.

They loaded their arms with wonderful gifts, and came before Mary and Joseph and the child. For some time, they paid homage to the infant Jesus and placed their precious treasures at his feet. Then they planned to return to Herod with the news of Jesus' whereabouts. But as they slept, that night, an angel appeared to each of them in a dream and warned them of Herod's plan. Quickly, the wise men loaded their horses and left the land of Judea, so that Herod could not find them.

That same night, an angel appeared to Joseph and said:

"There is danger here. Take Mary and the baby, and flee into Egypt, for Herod means to murder the child."

Indeed, King Herod was filled with wrath, for the wise men had not returned, and the baby's whereabouts still remained unknown to him. He then conceived a terrible plan.

"I must find this child and destroy him," he thought. "If every baby under two years of age is killed, then surely this child will be among them."

So he ordered his soldiers to slaughter hundreds of innocent children in Bethlehem. By this time, however, Jesus was safely on his way to Egypt in the arms of his mother.

There, in Egypt, the Holy Family stayed for a time. Then word came that the evil Herod was dead. Joseph knew he could safely return to Judea. But, instead of going to Bethlehem, Joseph led his family north to the hills of Galilee and the town of Nazareth, where he and Mary had lived before. Thus, they avoided Herod's son, who was now the king in Jerusalem and who was just as wicked as his father had been.

Jesus as a Boy

IN NAZARETH, Joseph followed his trade as a carpenter. His shop was next to the house where Mary and the baby Jesus spent the day. But, as Jesus grew up, it came time for him to learn his father's trade. Often, he would help Joseph at the carpenter's bench, planing wood and mending chairs.

Besides learning a trade, Jesus went to school. Every Jewish boy was obliged to learn the Torah, or the Five Books of Moses, so that he might fully obey the laws of God. Jesus found this training very easy. He "waxed strong in spirit, filled with wisdom," as the Gospel says.

On the Sabbath and on holidays, Jesus and Joseph went to the synagogue in Nazareth to pray and study. Once again, Jesus proved most learned and devout. When he was twelve years old, his parents decided to take him to Jerusalem for the Passover festival.

Jesus had been in Jerusalem as a tiny baby, but he remembered nothing of the great city and the awesome Temple. Now, for the first time, he gazed upon the place that had been home to King David and King Solomon. His heart was filled with the love of God.

Many times before, the boy Jesus had felt a strong passion for God and for religion. But it seems that he was not yet aware of his role in the world. From what we know, neither Mary nor Joseph, nor any of the angels of God came to him and told him, "You are the Saviour." It was Jesus' task to learn this himself, as he lived and suffered like any other man. Nevertheless, by the time he was twelve, he *had* discovered one most important truth: that all good men might call themselves the sons of God and live a perfect and righteous life by doing as God would do if He Himself lived on earth.

In Jerusalem, Jesus spent little time at the festivities. Instead, he went to the Temple, and entered the study rooms where many learned rabbis and aged teachers sat conversing and discussing the Law. To their amazement, this mere youth of twelve

seemed quite well versed in the teachings of Moses. After a while they sat in surprise as he instructed them on the deeper meanings and the inner truths of what he knew in his heart.

Mary and Joseph did not know that Jesus was in the Temple conversing with the priests and teachers. Nervously, they searched for him in the streets where the other boys were playing. But he could not be found. Nightfall was coming.

"Let us look in the Temple," said Joseph wearily.

There in the midst of the learned men, sat Jesus, discussing the most difficult points of religion.

"How worried we were," his mother said to him. "We did not know where to find you."

Jesus was surprised.

"Where else should I be," he said, "but in my Father's house, attending to His business?"

Mary was puzzled. She did not understand that Jesus referred to God as his father and had meant no insult to Joseph. The three returned silently to Nazareth. For many years Jesus led a quiet life, studying, growing wise, and every day coming nearer to the truth of his great identity.

The Gospels of Matthew, Mark, Luke, and John   *345*

The Baptism of Jesus

YOUNG JOHN GREW into manhood, and was filled with great religious fervor. Later, when he was about thirty years old, he went into the desert of Judea and lived alone, wearing a rough coat of camel's hair and eating only locusts and honey. His beard grew long, and his eyes shone with inspiration.

Occasionally, hecklers and wicked men came to make fun of John. He always knew when they were present, and raising his voice, he would cry:

"Repent! For the kingdom of Heaven is at hand!"

Because of his zeal, many thought that John was the Messiah. But the strange prophet always disclaimed that great distinction.

"I am not worthy to untie the laces of His sandals," he would say. "I am only His prophet, and I lead the way."

Nevertheless, hundreds of Jews, seeking comfort from their sorrows, followed John and joined him in the worship of God. To purify their souls and to wash away their sins, John instructed them to immerse themselves in the cold, clear waters of the River Jordan. This was the act of baptism, and, as a result, people called the prophet of the Lord, John the Baptist.

One day, as John was baptizing some of his followers, Jesus, now about thirty years old, came from Galilee to the River Jordan. Though Jesus and John were cousins, they had met only as children, for John spent most of his life in the desert. Nevertheless, the prophet recognized Jesus at once. Falling on his knees, he exclaimed:

"Behold! This is the One greater than I who will cleanse the world of its sins!"

Everyone was amazed. But Jesus said nothing. He advanced to the shore of the river and asked John to baptize him.

"*You* must baptize me," said John in reverence.

Jesus insisted, for he wished to know the experiences of all other men. So John baptized Jesus with the waters of the Jordan; and, as he did so, the clouds in the sky drew apart, a great burst of sunlight filled the scene, and, high above, a voice from heaven could be heard proclaiming:

"This is My beloved Son, in whom I am well pleased."

The Gospels of Matthew, Mark, Luke, and John   346

The Temptation of Jesus

NOW, MORE THAN EVER, the Holy Spirit filled Jesus, and he realized his mission in life. In order to prepare and purify his soul, he went into seclusion for forty days, deep within the barren wilderness of Judea.

While Jesus was fasting and at his prayers, Satan, the devil, came up from the lower depths to tempt and torture him.

"You think you are the Son of God," Satan said. "Then prove it to me. Turn these stones into loaves of bread and ease your hunger."

But Jesus remained at his prayers and quietly said:

"My prayers are more important to me, for man shall not live by bread alone."

The devil laughed.

"Well then," he said. "If you are really the Son of God, throw yourself off the highest steeple of the Temple, and we will see if you are saved."

Jesus remained at his prayers and simply said:

"It is wrong to test God's powers by such a reckless act."

The devil was becoming impatient. Intent upon trapping Jesus and ruining his soul, he devised another plan.

"Worship me!" he pleaded, "and I will make you master over all the cities of the world, and over all the wealth within those cities."

Then, through his magic trickery, Satan caused an image of all the glittering

The Gospels of Matthew, Mark, Luke, and John

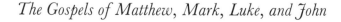

cities of the world to appear in the barren desert.

Jesus did not hesitate a minute. Sternly, he exclaimed,

"Away, Satan, away! God and only God will I serve!"

With these strong words, the devil was cast down to the lower depths whence he had come. Then the angels of God descended and brought food and comfort to Jesus, who had proved, beyond all doubt, his purity and his love of God.

When he was refreshed, Jesus prepared to return to the River Jordan to find his cousin John. But then he heard some sorry news. The new king Herod had arrested John for preaching against the sins of Herod's wicked wife. John was now in prison, perhaps being readied to die.

Jesus knew that it was best for him to return to Galilee and begin his ministry. He went to Capernaum near Nazareth. There he preached in the synagogue to the poor of the town.

"Repent!" he announced, "for the Kingdom of Heaven is at hand!"

Jesus and His Followers

AFTER THE ARREST of John the Baptist, many of John's followers went into hiding. They were alone, now that their leader had gone. But some of the men remembered Jesus of Galilee, and recalled that John had said:

"This is the One greater than I."

John had also referred to Jesus as the "Lamb of God," which meant that Jesus would take upon himself the sins and sufferings of the world, like a lamb sacrificed upon the altar.

The followers of John who remembered these things were now prepared to follow Jesus.

Two of these men, Andrew and Simon, were brothers who earned their living as fishermen on the sea of Galilee. One day, as Jesus was walking by the shores and meditating, he saw these brothers casting their nets into the waters.

The Gospels of Matthew, Mark, Luke, and John

Andrew recognized Jesus and was eager to follow him, but Simon was more reserved. As they were talking, a group of men and women came to the shore to hear Jesus preach. Often, persons met in out-of-the-way places to listen to this young man of Nazareth, who seemed so filled with authority and holiness.

That day, the crowd was very large. Jesus turned to Simon and asked him if he might stand in the fishing boat, so that everyone could see him and hear better. Simon agreed.

After the sermon, when the crowd had dispersed, Jesus advised Simon to row out a bit farther and lower his nets. There he would find many fish, which Simon need-ed, for he had not been lucky in his catch that day. Simon followed this advice. To his amazement, he caught so many fish that his net was full and his boat so heavy that it almost sank. The following day, when he saw Jesus, Simon threw himself on the ground and cried:

"I am a sinful man because I hesitated to follow you. Now I know that you are the one for whom we have all been waiting, and I wish to do your bidding."

Jesus helped Simon to his feet and told him to come with him and with Andrew and the others who were eager to find salvation.

"I will make you fishers of men," he said.

Now the word spread that the teacher Jesus of Nazareth was calling the faithful to abandon their old lives and follow him to bring the message of God to the world. John and James, the two sons of a man named Zebedee, joined the group, to be followed by Philip and a man named Nathanael. In time, they were all to be known as the disciples, or those who teach. Tirelessly, they toured the cities of Galilee with Jesus, spreading the word of God.

The Wedding at Cana

IN THE SMALL TOWN of Cana, there was to be a wedding. Among the honored guests were Jesus, his mother, and several of the disciples. In those days, a wedding feast took many days, and much food and wine was consumed.

Jesus only attended briefly, for he was busy preaching. He arrived toward the end of the feast, when all the wine had been drunk. Mary was a close friend of the host. She knew that he was greatly embarrassed to have no more wine, since an important official from the city was coming to pay his respects.

So Mary turned to her son, Jesus, and said:

"I know that you possess great powers. Can you help these friends? They have no wine and they expect an important guest."

Jesus had not yet performed any of the miracles that lay in his power. He did not wish to attract a following of those who would be impressed only with magic and sorcery, for his message appealed to the soul. Nevertheless, out of respect for his

mother, Jesus decided to help. He told the servants to fetch six large pitchers.

"Fill them with water from the well," he said.

The servants obeyed. Jesus had them carry the pitchers to the table. By this time, the high official of the city had arrived and was asking for a glass of wine.

The guests knew that there was no wine, and were amused when the servants brought the water pitchers to the table. But, to their amazement, when the colorless water was poured it turned into clear red wine. Everyone filled his cup and drank.

"Wonderful!" said the high official. "This is the finest wine I have ever tasted."

All the guests agreed, and complimented the host for saving the best wine until last. But the disciples of Jesus knew that a real miracle had occurred, and their faith and reverence increased.

Jesus Preaches and Heals the Sick

NOW THAT HE HAD changed the water to wine, Jesus was becoming famous in the area of Nazareth. He journeyed with his disciples to Capernaum again, and there he preached in the synagogue. It was the custom for learned men to give sermons and read lessons on the holidays.

While Jesus was preaching, a man in the congregation started to shout and call out insults and blasphemies. This man was unhappy and ill, but the people of the village simply thought he was insane and paid him no mind. Jesus came down from the pulpit, where he was preaching, and gently placed his hand on the angry man's shoulders. Then he lifted his eyes to God, and, soon, the man who had been shouting, his

The Gospels of Matthew, Mark, Luke, and John

face red with rage, became quiet and calm. Everyone was deeply impressed, and the word spread fast that Jesus had the power to heal the sick with prayer.

Simon, the fisherman, who had joined the disciples, was in need of Jesus' help. His mother-in-law lay ill with a serious fever and no doctor could relieve her. Jesus entered the house and straightaway cured the elderly woman. All the curious neighbors who had crowded into the house were overwhelmed with astonishment. But Jesus wanted no praise. He left the cured woman and went to a solitary place to pray. There Simon followed him and declared himself a faithful disciple forever-more. With Jesus, he journeyed through Galilee preaching in the synagogues.

But it is always true that a famous man gathers enemies as well as friends. Many men of power became jealous and angry at the news that Jesus of Nazareth could heal the sick and cause great multitudes to follow him and accept his ideas.

One day, Jesus was preaching in the streets, when he heard a commotion nearby. The people were hurrying away in all directions because a leper was coming. A leper is afflicted with a terrible disease that causes flaking and scabbing of the skin. In those days it was thought that this disease was very contagious, and lepers were not allowed to mingle with other people. But this poor man wanted to be cured, and he dared venture into the streets to find Jesus.

"Make me clean again," the leper pleaded, "for no one will help me, and my life is meaningless."

In his great compassion, Jesus stretched forth his hands and touched the leper on the head. In that instant the horrible disease miraculously disappeared. Now, more than ever, the people praised Jesus—but his enemies also hated him all the more.

Time after time, in many ways and in many places, Jesus stretched forth his hand and cured the lame, the blind, and the suffering. He became so popular, in spite of his wish, that people lined up for hours to gain admittance to the house or the street where he was preaching.

One day, he was visiting a small house in Galilee. Such a great crowd had gathered

The Gospels of Matthew, Mark, Luke, and John

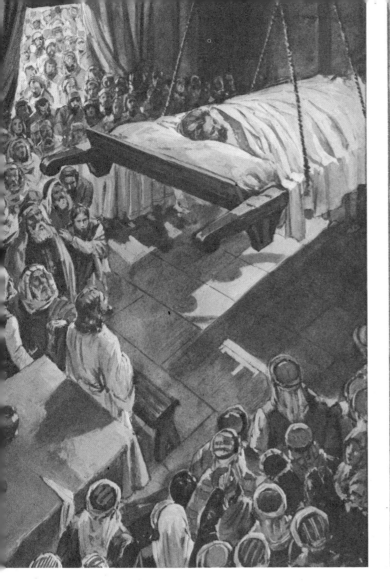

that no one could get in or out of the door. Outside some people had brought a sick man on his bed so that Jesus might cure him. Because they could not force their way in through the door, they decided to remove the roof and lower the invalid down, bed and all. Some of Jesus' enemies were watching. They were always prepared to make fun of Jesus or to cast doubts upon his wisdom and holiness. Now, when they saw the sick man being lowered on his bed, they laughed aloud.

But Jesus admired the resourcefulness of the invalid and his friends, and he blessed them and stretched forth his hands. The man who, for years, had been unable to rise from his bed, now walked and was cured. He was so well, in fact, that he lifted the bed on his back and marched out of the house, praising God.

Jesus' enemies were angry. What right did this carpenter's son have to take upon himself the powers of God and the ancient prophets? they asked. Deliberately, they started to spread the word that Jesus was actually a sinner, a man who purposely broke the laws of God. This was like saying that night was day and black was white. But many aristocrats thought that Jesus was becoming too powerful and too well loved by the poor and unhappy people of Judea.

The Gospels of Matthew, Mark, Luke, and John

The Calling of Matthew

JESUS WAS always looking for upright men who could help him spread the word of God. He had felt that Simon, the fisherman, was such a man. Now he saw Matthew, and he wished him to join the great cause.

But Matthew was not a fisherman or a farmer. He pursued a very unpopular profession, and it caused him to be disliked and hated, for Matthew was a tax collector. It was his duty, though a Jew himself, to round up money from the Jews so that it might be paid to Herod and to Rome. Matthew was not happy in his work, but he knew that someone had to do it. Being kind by nature, he was, at least, a pleasant tax collector, and never persecuted anyone.

It was Jesus' hope that he would attract a following of many different kinds of people; rich and poor, wise and simple, tax collectors as well as fishermen. One day, he approached the place where Matthew was counting taxes. Standing to the side, Jesus raised his arm and beckoned Matthew, saying:

"Follow me."

Matthew, a publican, as tax collectors were called, had heard of Jesus and believed in him. Without hesitation, he followed Jesus, and became a disciple. He invited other publicans to dine with Jesus.

Jesus' enemies were delighted with this latest piece of news. Imagine, they thought, now he has taken tax collectors into his company. Following Jesus to an inn, they confronted him and said:

"If you are a holy person sent by God, how can you sit here eating supper with tax collectors, beggars, and all sorts of common people?"

Jesus was never flustered by the question of his enemies. He smiled peacefully, and said:

"God has sent me to be a doctor to the sick. Why should I spend my time with those who are already well and sound? I must help the unhappy man, the hopeless man, and the sinner, whatever his calling or his station in life."

The Gospels of Matthew, Mark, Luke, and John

Thus Jesus spoke words and ideas that were new to the world, and, wherever he went, he gathered the sinners and the lowly, so that he might redeem them. But his detractors still complained.

"Why should God be concerned with sinners?" they asked.

And Jesus replied:

"God waits for all men to pay their debts to Him. The greater the debt, the greater the repentance, and the greater God's forgiveness."

To the fair-minded people of Judea, these words made sense. But the enemies of Jesus continued to argue and complain. When they heard that Jesus and his disciples had picked some grain to eat on the Sabbath day, they jumped on this infraction of the law, and cried out that Jesus had sinned. But the man from Nazareth simply reminded them that King David of old had done the same thing when he was hungry. David, in fact, had eaten the showbread meant for the rituals, yet the Lord did not punish him.

"That is all very well and good," said the enemies, "but you profane the Sabbath. You walk around preaching and do not go to the Temple."

Jesus answered quietly:

"A man need not be in the Temple to feel the presence of God, nor was man made just to worship on the Sabbath. The Sabbath was made for man."

Jesus' enemies even criticized him for curing the sick and suffering on the Sabbath. But Jesus explained:

"If you had a sheep and it fell into a pit on the Sabbath, you would not leave it there until the next day; by then it might be dead. Should we treat a sheep any better than we treat a man? No, God does not wish man to suffer needlessly, even on the Sabbath."

The enemies could not answer and turned away.

"This man Jesus must be destroyed," they whispered to themselves.

Jesus Visits Jerusalem

AT DIFFERENT TIMES in his life, Jesus visited the great city of Jerusalem in order to worship at the Temple. The favorite time for such a visit was at Passover, the great celebration of the Jewish Exodus from Egypt under Moses.

With several of his disciples, Jesus came into Jerusalem unnoticed in the great throng of holiday visitors. At another time, in the not-too-distant future, he was to enter the city again, triumphantly—and he was to die there as well. This Jesus knew in his heart, but he said nothing to his disciples.

There was a man in Jerusalem to whom Jesus confided some of the most important concepts of his faith and of his mission on earth. This man was Nicodemus, a wealthy and influential Jew. One night, Nicodemus secretly sought out Jesus in a quiet room.

"I have heard of your miracles," said Nicodemus, "and I have listened to you speak. I want to know more about what you believe."

For many hours Jesus talked to Nicodemus. He told him that man was capable of everlasting life in the Kingdom of God, that, to enter this Kingdom, man had to have a pure heart and faith in God. Then Jesus reminded Nicodemus of the time when Moses fashioned a snake out of brass so that those beholding it might be saved from the poisonous bites of real serpents. Such a miracle would take place again through the Son of God, who, like the brazen snake, would be suspended on a cross and die for the salvation of mankind. Jesus then revealed an amazing thing to Nicodemus.

"God so loved the world," he said, "that He gave His only begotten son, so that whoever believes in Him will not die, but will live forever."

Jesus did not say directly that he was the Son of God to Nicodemus—but, clearly, he was speaking of himself and envisioning the time of his own death and resurrection.

The visit with Nicodemus, including the discussion held that night, is one of the most important and meaningful events in the whole story of Jesus and his teachings.

The Woman at the Well

AFTER THE PASSOVER FEAST, Jesus journeyed back to Galilee. He took the long way home, and thus passed through the land of Samaria, a place not friendly to the Jews. Jesus had a purpose in doing this, for he wanted to spread the word of God to people other than the Jews. So he went to the well in the center of the town of Sychar and sat there to rest. Soon a

Samaritan woman came along to fetch some water.

"Would you give me a drink of water?" Jesus asked. The woman was surprised. Usually, Jews did not speak to Samaritans, let alone ask them for water.

"Why do you ask me?" she said.

"If you knew who I am," he answered, "you would ask me to give *you* the living waters that I possess."

The woman was confused. She wanted to know what waters he meant. Jesus said:

"Whoever drinks of ordinary water soon becomes thirsty again. But if you drink the waters I bring, you will never be thirsty again and you will have everlasting life."

The Samaritan woman became all excited. Naturally, she wanted some of this wonderful water, and asked Jesus to provide it. She did not understand that he was not speaking of real water, but of faith.

"First, you must purify your heart," said Jesus to the woman, "for I know that you are a sinner and have done some wicked things."

The woman blushed. It was true, she had been wicked. Realizing that she was talking to a religious prophet, the woman tried to excuse herself by saying:

"I am not a Jew, and I do not worship as you do."

Jesus assured her that the message and blessings of God were meant for all mankind, and that God had chosen the Jews as a means of bringing this salvation to the world.

"I know," the woman said. "I have heard that the Messiah called Christ will come from them—and that the whole world awaits him."

Jesus then spoke some startling words.

"I am he, the Messiah," he said.

The Samaritan woman was thus the first one to hear, directly from Jesus' own lips, these magnificent words. She immediately believed what she heard and rushed off to spread the news.

Jesus remained at the well. Soon some of his disciples came along with food, which they had purchased in the city.

But Jesus did not eat. His talk with the Samaritan woman had so filled his spirit that he felt no need of food. Later, he preached in Samaria at the well where he had revealed his divinity to the humble Samaritan woman.

The Sermon on the Mount

ALL OVER GALILEE, in Syria, to the north and to the south, the word of Jesus' powers and holiness was spreading. Multitudes of people came to hear the Master and to be cured by his outstretched hand. Though Jesus knew that this was his role on earth, he nevertheless shunned the praises and adulation of the crowds. Often, he would stand in a small boat at the water's edge while the people listened from the shore. Then he would preach and heal, and, straightaway, he would leave the scene to meditate by himself in the hills.

To assist in his great work, Jesus appointed twelve of his followers to be apostles, and thus to possess the powers of healing and the insight to preach the Word of God. These apostles were Simon the fisherman, who was later called Peter; Andrew, his brother; James and John, the sons of Zebedee; Philip; Bartholomew; Thomas; Matthew the tax collector; James Alpheus; Thaddeus; Simon from Canaan; and a man named Judas Iscariot. These twelve preached to the people, as Jesus had instructed them.

Then one day, as he was meditating, Jesus saw thousands of people wending their way up the side of the mountain so that they might hear him preach. He called his disciples and told them to prepare the throng, for he would make a sermon there on the mountain, and, in this sermon, he would say all those things that mankind had to know for its salvation. The undying words he spoke that day are beyond compare in all history. He said:

> Blessed are the poor in spirit:
>   for theirs is the kingdom of heaven.
> Blessed are they that mourn:
>   for they shall be comforted.
> Blessed are the meek:
>   for they shall inherit the earth.
> Blessed are they which do hunger
>   and thirst after righteousness:
>   for they shall be filled.
> Blessed are the merciful:
>   for they shall obtain mercy.
> Blessed are the pure in heart:
>   for they shall see God.
> Blessed are the peacemakers:
>   for they shall be called the
>   children of God.
> Blessed are they which are
>   persecuted for righteousness' sake:
>   for theirs is the kingdom
>   of heaven.
> Blessed are ye, when men shall
>   revile you, and persecute you,
>   and shall say all manner of evil
>   against you falsely, for my sake.
> Rejoice and be exceeding glad: for
>   great is your reward in heaven:
>   for so persecuted they the
>   prophets which were before you.

The blessings that Jesus pronounced are called the Beatitudes. They were the first part of his Sermon on the Mount. In the second part, Jesus went on to assure the Jews that his task was not to upset the Laws of Moses, but, rather, to fulfill them. For that reason he recited the famous Golden Rule: *Do unto others as you would have them do unto you.*

He also gave the humble and the poor great hope and courage, for he told them that they did not need wealth and high station to enter the kingdom of God, but, rather, righteousness and purity. Recalling the Ten Commandments, he warned that if we hate a man without cause and wish him dead, it is as if we murder him. He then urged the people to be merciful and forgiving, even with their enemies, and he said:

"Whosoever shall smite thee on thy right cheek, turn to him the other, also."

By this he meant: do not hastily strike back at someone who attacks you, but, rather, show him the peaceful intentions of your heart.

Furthermore, Jesus inspired the people to believe that God was always with them. They did not need the Temple, he said, or the synagogue, or the elaborate rituals of their religion to feel the presence of God and to become holy. Instead of repetitious prayers and chantings, Jesus taught a simple prayer, which all men might offer, for he said:

"Your Father in Heaven knows what is in your hearts."

The words he pronounced are called the Lord's Prayer, the most beautiful prayer in all the world:

> Our Father which art in heaven,
> Hallowed be thy name.
> Thy kingdom come.
> > Thy will be done in earth,
> > as it is in heaven.

Give us this day our daily bread.
And forgive us our debts,
   as we forgive our debtors.
And lead us not into temptation,
   but deliver us from evil:
For Thine is the kingdom, and the power,
   and the glory, for ever. Amen.

After this, Jesus spoke many more immortal words, and taught the meaning of faith and love, of justice, and salvation. Then he departed, and left the people astonished and inspired beyond all their dreams.

The Gospels of Matthew, Mark, Luke, and John   *365*

Jesus Saves Two Young Men

IN THE CITY of Capernaum there were about one hundred Roman soldiers stationed to keep the peace. At the head of this small army was a centurion, or a captain, as we would call him. He lived very well and had many servants, one of whom became quite ill. The centurion loved this servant like a son, and was distressed to see him suffering without hope of being cured.

Jesus was in Capernaum, and the centurion sent word beseeching him to save his dying servant. The disciples told Jesus that this Roman had been very kind to the Jews, and that he had even helped them build their synagogue. Jesus went to the centurion's house immediately. But as he approached, the centurion's messengers came running down the stairs with a note from their master. It said:

"Lord, I do not feel worthy enough to have you honor my house, nor do I think myself worthy to appear in person before you. But I have great faith that you can cure

The Gospels of Matthew, Mark, Luke, and John   *366*

my servant without seeing him, even as I command many soldiers whom I do not know. I beg you to show mercy."

Jesus was deeply impressed with such faith. Moreover, he rejoiced to see that people other than the Jews were accepting his teachings and his power. He prayed for the dying man. That night, the centurion found that a miracle had taken place, and that his servant was well.

In the city of Nain, a poor widow was in grief. Her only son, her hope and support, had died of a fever. Jesus came to see the widow and found her kneeling beside the bed on which her son's body was laid. With great compassion, Jesus stretched forth his hand and called out:

"Young man, arise and live."

To everyone's amazement the boy who had been dead arose as one awakes in the morning, and embraced his mother. Soon the entire country heard about this miracle, and many, many more people began to believe that Jesus of Nazareth was indeed the Saviour of whom the prophets had spoken.

Yet many also doubted and hated Jesus. Some were sincere, others merely wicked. The followers of John the Baptist were honest in their doubts of Jesus, for they believed John to be the Messiah. After all, they said, John lived a life of pain and suffering in the desert; he never ate meat or drank wine; he now awaits death in Herod's prison. Is he not the real Messiah?

Jesus understood their doubts.

"You can't imagine that the Saviour should come to you neatly dressed, eating with tax collectors, going to weddings, and drinking wine. But God is wise, and knows what He is doing."

Then he continued:

"Come unto me, all you that labor and are heavy laden, and I will give you rest."

The Rejection in Nazareth and the Sinful Woman

JESUS WAS ESPECIALLY anxious to preach in Nazareth, where he had spent most of his life. There his mother Mary lived and his father, Joseph the carpenter, was buried. One day, Jesus asked permission to preach in the synagogue at Nazareth, and, according to custom, he was invited to do so.

Taking the Book of the Law in his hand, Jesus read about his own ministry among the poor and suffering, just as the prophets had described it many hundreds of years before. Though Jesus was very convincing in his speech, the elders of the synagogue in Nazareth rejected him.

"Isn't this the carpenter's son?" they asked in ridicule. "Is he trying to say that he is the Messiah of whom the prophets wrote?" And they laughed.

Jesus' disciples were unhappy to see their master rejected, especially in his own home town. But Jesus was philosophical.

"No prophet is accepted in his own country," he said. "Therefore, we must preach among other people. After all, you remember how Elisha, the prophet, converted Naaman, a man from Syria. God wishes us to spread His word among all the people of the world."

So they went on their way, preaching and teaching in the nearby towns. As usual, the enemies of Jesus followed close behind. They hoped to trap Jesus in public, so that the people would no longer believe in him. For this purpose, they brought a sinful woman into his presence. This woman had been taken in adultery—a crime that was punishable by stoning, according to the ancient laws.

"What would you do with this wicked woman?" shouted Jesus' enemies. Jesus was silent at first. He stooped down and wrote something in the sand at his feet.

The enemies smiled. They thought they had truly trapped Jesus. If he said that the

The Gospels of Matthew, Mark, Luke, and John

368

sinful woman should go free, they could accuse him of disobeying the sacred laws. And if he condemned the woman and had her stoned to death, they could say that he was cruel and without mercy.

Jesus sought neither path. He rose and said simply:

"He that is without sin among you, let him cast the first stone at her."

Everyone was amazed. For in that crowd there was no one without sin—and no one worthy of condemning another human being. One by one, the conscience-stricken people left the scene until Jesus was alone with the sinful woman.

"We must not condemn each other," said Jesus to the woman. "We must forgive and pray to be forgiven. Go then, and sin no more."

The sinful woman was so grateful to Jesus that she became one of his followers. Some believe that this was Mary of Magdala, or Mary Magdalene. It is also said that, one night, while Jesus was dining in a rich man's house, Mary Magdalene entered with rare spices and oil so that she might anoint Jesus' feet. In those days, people always removed their shoes when they went inside, and bathed their feet and sprinkled them with fine spices and oils.

Magdalene anointed Jesus' feet with her tears and dried them with the hair of her

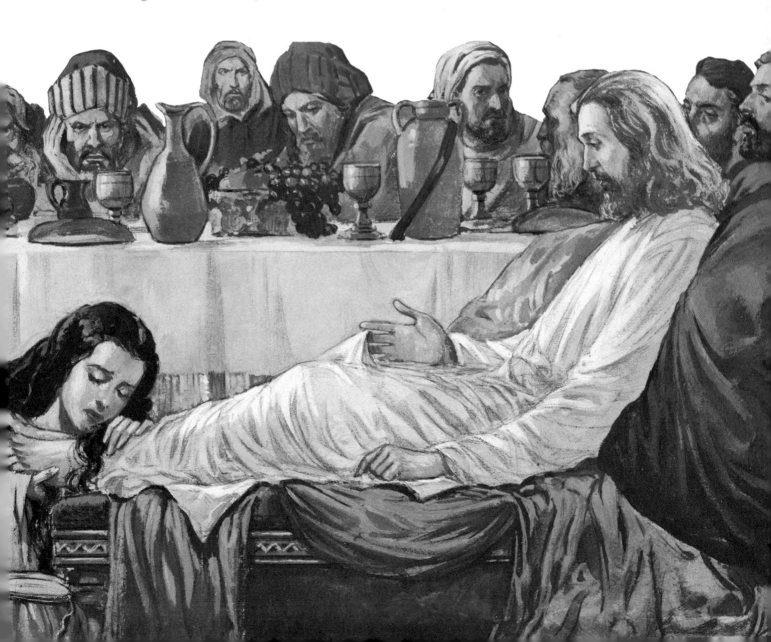

head. Then she sprinkled them with spices and oil. The rich man at whose table Jesus was dining watched all this in surprise, and wondered how Jesus could allow a woman of such bad reputation to touch him, let alone anoint his feet.

Jesus spoke softly and reminded his host that God forgives all sinners who repent; the greater the sin, the greater is the repentance and the greater God's forgiveness.

"You are a rich man," said Jesus to his host. "But when I came into your house tonight, you did not anoint my feet and sprinkle them with spices and oil. You think your sins are few and you need not repent. But this woman knows her sins, and they are great. Thus will she be forgiven."

Then Jesus told a parable, to illustrate his point. Two men owed money to another man. One owed five hundred pieces of silver, the other only fifty. The man to whom the money was owed was generous and disclaimed both debts. Which of the debtors do you think was most appreciative? asked Jesus. And the rich host answered:

"The man who owed five hundred pieces of silver."

"Exactly," Jesus replied, "He who is forgiven the most will love the most. Just as this woman whom I forgave loves me and believes in me more than you do."

Jesus Answers His Enemies

NO MATTER HOW KINDLY Jesus spoke and how wisely he proved his teachings, his enemies taunted him and tried to cast doubts upon his mission. They began to spread the rumor that Jesus was in league with the devil himself, because he cured people and brought them back from death. They argued that, since the devil brought about disease and suffering, only the devil could call them off.

Jesus answered boldly:

"How can Satan cast out Satan?" he asked. "If a house is divided against itself, that house cannot stand. The fact is that God and only God can undo the devil's treachery, and you who are evil at heart cannot know good or speak wisely."

Then Jesus spoke of Jonah, who had been three days in the belly of a whale.

"So shall the Son of Man be three days in the heart of the earth," said Jesus. But no one grasped the meaning of these prophetic words.

In the crowd listening to Jesus were Mary, his mother, and his brothers and sisters. When someone pointed them out to him, Jesus exclaimed:

"All people are my brothers and sisters, for all of us have the same Father, who is God in heaven."

Parables of the Sower and the Kingdom of God

JESUS WAS A GREAT TEACHER because he made his lessons clear and easily understandable. To do this, he often told parables, or stories with a message. One day, while standing in a boat on the shores of Galilee, Jesus told this story to the crowd:

A farmer filled his apron with seeds, and set off to scatter them in the fresh earth. As he tossed the seeds this way and that way, some fell by the wayside, where the blackbirds ate them; some fell upon stony places; some fell among the brambles; and others fell into the earth, as they were supposed to. Jesus explained the story to his disciples.

"My words are like the seeds," he said. "Some will fall by the wayside and be ignored, so that the devil, like a blackbird, will come and eat them up. Some will fall upon people who are like rocks where no seed can take root, and therefore perishes. My words will also fall among brambles—among people who are too caught up with other things,

such as money and pleasure, to concern themselves with the teachings of God. And my words will also fall upon those people, who, like fresh earth, are ready and willing to accept them and let them grow and bear fruit. This is the meaning of my parable.''

Jesus often used the example of seeds being scattered in the fields as a way of clarifying his message. He knew that many of the people who listened to him were farmers and would understand the comparisons. Once, he compared heaven to a mustard seed, which is the least imposing of all seeds until it grows. Then it becomes a great tree, with many branches upon which many birds may live.

The Great Storm at Sea

AFTER TELLING his parables, Jesus decided it was time to travel, and he beckoned his disciples to follow him across the sea of Galilee to the distant shore. They all boarded a ship, which then set sail.

Jesus was weary. He stretched out on the deck and soon fell fast asleep. As the ship made its way across the sea, a ferocious storm began brewing in the heavens. Within minutes, thunder and lightning were striking, and great waves were tossing the ship without mercy.

The disciples became fearful of their lives. Rushing to Jesus, they roused him from his sleep, crying:

"Save us, Master, save us!"

Without hesitation, Jesus lifted his arms and ordered the heavens to be at peace. In that same instant, the storm subsided and the great waves disappeared, so that the sea was peaceful and calm. Then Jesus turned to his friends and said:

"Why did you doubt that you would be saved? If I am with you, and you believe in me, then you will never perish."

The disciples, who knew Jesus and had seen his miracles before, were nonetheless amazed that he could command the very heavens themselves to obey.

When the ship docked on the far side of the sea, Jesus beheld a poor, sick man wandering in the graveyards of the countryside. This man, long afflicted with madness, had been abandoned by his family and friends. Now he was alone and he could do nothing but cause himself harm.

Jesus aproached this piteous person and asked his name.

The man replied:

"My name is Legion."

By this, he meant that there were many sorry souls like him throughout the world possessed by many demons. Jesus lifted his hands and ordered the evil spirits out of the man and into the bodies of some swine that were feeding nearby. Then these swine ran, possessed, into the sea and disappeared.

Now the man whose name was Legion was cured, and he begged to join the disciples. But Jesus urged him to stay among his own people and spread the word of God, for the people would believe him, seeing him cured and having known how hopeless he once had been.

Jairus' Daughter

JESUS AND THE DISCIPLES returned to Capernaum aboard their ship. This time the sea was calm. But upon the shore a great crowd awaited with excitement, for many had come to be healed.

Most eager in the crowd was Jairus, a high official of the synagogue. His twelve-year-old daughter lay dying, and he knew that only Jesus could save her. As the Master set foot on the shore, Jairus rushed forward and begged Jesus to hasten to his house and save his child. Jesus immediately responded and started to make his way through the crowd.

Waiting on a side road was an elderly woman who had suffered from a blood disease for many years. Countless doctors had been unable to help her; now she knew that Jesus was her only hope. But, as he passed, the crowd was so thick that she could not speak to him. Hurriedly she followed behind, having faith that to touch the hem of his robe would be enough to cure her illness. With great effort, the elderly woman managed to place her fingers just at the hem of the Master's robe.

Though hundreds of people pressed in from every side, Jesus knew that someone in need of him had touched his robe. He stopped.

"Who touched me?" he inquired.

"Everyone is touching you," his disciples replied, "for the crowd is very large."

"Yes," said Jesus, "but there is someone here who was ill and now she is healed, for I felt my curative powers entering her soul."

The sickly woman fearfully raised her hand and admitted that she had touched the Master. Jesus was pleased.

"So great is this woman's faith," he said, "that she need but touch my robe to be healed."

At this same moment a messenger came running toward Jairus with the ter-

rible news that his daughter had died. The poor man broke down in tears. But Jesus spoke words of comfort.

"Only believe," he said, "and all will be well."

Then Jesus hastened to Jairus' house, where many people were mourning and weeping.

"She is dead," they said to Jesus. "Why try to save her now?"

"She is not dead," Jesus replied. "She is merely asleep."

Though the others were scornful, he went to the little girl's bed and commanded her to rise. Miraculously, the child opened her eyes and walked from her bed into the arms of her joyous parents.

"Give her something to eat," said Jesus, "and tell no one of this miracle. I do not perform these deeds in order to win praise, but to prove the power of God."

After this, Jesus journeyed through the streets, and blind men and deaf mutes followed him and cried out their faith in his powers, so that they were cured. From Capernaum to the shores of Galilee, in the cities beyond, the word spread fast; no one had ever seen such miracles as the miracles of Jesus.

The Disciples Are Instructed
and Many Persons Are Fed

TIME WAS SHORT and Jesus had a great deal of work to do. In order to spread the word of God, he instructed his twelve disciples in the purposes of his mission and he endowed them with the miraculous power of healing.

"Heal the sick, cleanse the lepers, raise the dead, cast out devils," he said, "and ask nothing in return."

The Gospels of Matthew, Mark, Luke, and John   *376*

He further warned them to be very careful.

"I send you forth as sheep in the midst of wolves," he said. "Therefore, be as wise as serpents and as harmless as doves."

The disciples were inspired, and set off for many distant cities in order to heal and preach in the manner of Jesus.

Weeks later, the disciples joined Jesus again. They saw how hard he had worked and urged him to rest. But, as he went up to a quiet place in order to sit beneath a shade tree, he found a great throng of people awaiting him.

"They are like sheep without a shepherd," said Jesus, and, forgetting his own need of rest, he went into the midst of the crowd and preached.

By evening, more people had joined the throng, and all were hungry. The disciples thought that it was time to send them home to eat.

"No," said Jesus. "They are poor and we must feed them."

"But we have only a few pennies," answered the disciples, "not enough for even a small loaf of bread."

Jesus looked around. Seated nearby was a boy with a picnic basket. In the basket

The Gospels of Matthew, Mark, Luke, and John   377

were five loaves of bread and two small fish. Jesus took the food and performed a great miracle. With only five loaves of bread and two little fish, he was able to feed five thousand people, and, when they were done eating, there were twelve baskets of food left over.

The throng was astonished. They wanted to make Jesus king and put him on a throne. But Jesus wished no such earthly praise, and he quietly left the scene and disappeared into the hills.

Jesus Walks on the Water

AFTER THE MIRACLE of the loaves and fishes, Jesus instructed his disciples to cross the Sea of Galilee, so that they might continue their preaching. He stood on the shore bidding them good-by as they set sail.

However, when night fell, the sea became very rough, and the disciples had a hard time rowing the boat. Suddenly, they saw a figure apparently walking on the water. At

first, they were afraid, because it was dark and they could not recognize their Master. But, once Jesus made himself known, they rejoiced.

Peter had doubted that anyone could walk on the sea, and asked Jesus to endow him with the same power. Stepping out of the boat at Jesus' bidding, Peter found that he could also walk upon the waves. But, suddenly, a wind blew up and Peter became afraid, thus losing faith. Immediately, he began to sink. Jesus rescued him, saying:

"Man of little faith, why did you doubt?"

Peter was ashamed, but now, more than ever, he was convinced of his Master's divinity. Later, Jesus sat among his disciples and asked them:

"Who do you think I really am?"

Some said that he was the prophet Jeremiah, reborn, or Isaiah, or even Elijah. But Peter said:

"You are Christ, the Son of the Living God."

Jesus was deeply impressed with Peter's understanding and faith, and he said to him:

"You, Peter, are the rock upon which I will build my church, and you will also sit at the gates of heaven and hold the keys to my kingdom in your hands."

The other disciples now realized that their Master was indeed the Messiah, the Christ, for whom the world had prayed. But Jesus warned them not to speak of this news in public.

The Mission of Mercy Continues

FOR MANY MONTHS, Jesus and his disciples traveled through Galilee and other parts of the Holy Land, curing the sick, preaching, and debating their ideas. Jesus made no distinction among the suffering. Jews and gentiles (or foreigners) were healed by him. Children and old people came to be comforted; the blind and deaf, the sick in body and mind, all were saved by faith in his word and teachings.

But, still, the scribes and the Pharisees and the rulers of the cities believed Jesus to be a dangerous and troublesome man. In spite of the proofs of his power, these enemies of Jesus continued to plan ways to ensnare and perhaps destroy him.

Yet he continued his work. One day, at the city of Bethsaida, Jesus restored a blind man's sight. Later, he healed an epileptic boy.

Jesus also continued to instruct his disciples in the ways of the Lord. It was important that they be able to answer their enemies, so that the people would respect their wisdom.

Once a tax collector stopped Peter, and said to him:

"You are a follower of Jesus, and he says many things about the proper way to live; but, tell me, does he pay his taxes?"

Peter immediately answered, "Yes."

Nevertheless, Peter wondered if Jesus, a divine being from God, should actually have to pay taxes, for a king did not pay taxes in Judea. He asked Jesus about this, and Jesus replied:

"I will pay the tax and keep the peace. We want no trouble over such a little matter."

"Very well," said Peter, "but there is no money to pay the tax."

"Go to the sea," said Jesus, "and cast your line."

Peter did so. The first fish he caught had a coin in its mouth. Peter took the coin, sought out the tax collector and said:

"Here is my master's tax."

Thus, the disciples learned the proper conduct of their lives. But they learned the hard way.

One day, they were arguing among themselves about which one of them was the most important and would, thus, receive the most reward in Jesus' eyes. Overhearing this foolish argument, Jesus said:

"If any man desires to be first in the kingdom of heaven then he must really be last; he must be humble, serve others, do good things, and expect no reward. But he who thinks of himself as great and righteous and expects glory, he shall be considered lowly in the eyes of God."

Jesus then prophesied his own death and said that many would come after him who would take up the burden of his work and suffer the same fate, but that they who did so and died for the cause would gain eternal life in heaven.

"What does a man profit if he gains the whole world," said Jesus, "but gives up his chance to live after death?"

The Transfiguration

SOMETHING JESUS HAD SAID troubled the disciples, and they spoke of it among themselves.

"What did he mean about his death and resurrection?" they asked.

Several times now, Jesus had made reference to a time, not far off, when he would go to Jerusalem, be condemned, and later be forced to carry a weighty cross upon which he would die. Then, Jesus said, he would rise from the dead, after three days, to show all the world God's great mercy and power. The disciples could not understand the mystery and wonder of these prophecies.

Jesus did not explain further. One night, he asked three of his followers, Peter, John, and James, to walk with him to a high mountain in the north country. He wanted to pray there.

The three men walked with Jesus and became weary. When they reached the peak, they lay down, wrapped their cloaks about them, and slept. Jesus, meanwhile, knelt in prayer. Then a wonderful thing happened: the heavens opened, a great light poured forth, and two mighty figures appeared, from the clouds above the peak. They were Moses and Elijah, the great ancient prophets of God. They had come to speak with Jesus, the Messiah.

The bright light and the glory of this moment roused Peter and his friends from their sleep. When Peter saw the figures of Moses and Elijah and the transfiguration of Jesus into a being of radiance and great beauty, he fell on his knees and cried out:

"Let me build a temple here to commemorate this great moment." But, as he spoke, a voice was heard far above, saying:

"Behold, this is My beloved Son in whom I am well pleased. Believe in him, and that is enough."

When Peter raised his head, the vision had disappeared, leaving Jesus in a glowing light. Now, more than ever, Peter and his friends knew that their Master was the Son of God; in other words, God in the form of man. But Jesus advised them to keep this knowledge to themselves. Again, he foresaw his fate in Jerusalem, but he comforted his disciples, saying:

"Even my death is part of God's great plan."

The Good Samaritan

THE TEACHING of God's word was now going forth with great speed. Jesus appointed seventy righteous men to visit seventy cities in order to preach. Others took up the task of healing: and many evil spirits were cast out of the land.

Still Jesus' enemies tried to ensnare him. One day a lawyer stood up and called

out to Jesus:

"How shall I achieve eternal life? What is the way?"

And Jesus answered:

"You shall love the Lord your God with all your heart, and you shall love your neighbor as yourself."

The lawyer was cunning, and he said:

"Love my neighbor? How do I know who my neighbor is? Suppose he is a stranger to me?"

To answer this insincere question, Jesus told a parable, as follows:

Once a certain man was journeying from Jerusalem to Jericho, when he was suddenly attacked by robbers, who left him badly beaten and stripped by the side of the road. As the poor man lay there, a high-and-mighty priest rode by. Seeing the suffering man, he turned his face and quickly galloped away. He wanted no part of any trouble. Similarly, a Levite, one of the officials of the Temple, came by, looked at the injured man, and also hurried off without trying to help.

Then a humble man from Samaria, a Samaritan as he was called, journeyed by and, seeing the wounded man, rushed to his aid, and carefully dressed his injuries. Then the Samaritan lifted him onto his horse and took him to a nearby inn to recuperate. Moreover, when morning dawned, the Samaritan gave the unfortunate man some money, so that he might find his way home.

Now Jesus asked to the lawyer:

"Which of the three men would you consider the neighbor of the injured man?"

And the lawyer answered:

"The Samaritan, because he helped him and showed him mercy."

"Indeed," said Jesus, "we are all neighbors if we show mercy to each other. Now you go and do the same."

The Man Born Blind

A POOR BEGGAR lay in the streets, blind and helpless. Jesus was passing, and took pity on the man, who begged for comfort. Taking some clay from the ground, Jesus moistened it and applied it to the blind man's eyes. Then he told him to wash himself in the pool at Siloam, nearby.

The beggar obeyed, and, when he had finished bathing, he found his sight restored and his whole body well and straight. He returned to his home to declare the wondrous miracles of Jesus. But his neighbors were suspicious. They didn't believe that this healthy-looking man was the same beggar whom they had seen every day lying in the streets.

Jesus' enemies took advantage of the situation. They implied that the so-called blind man was a fraud. Some people sought out the beggar's parents and asked them, "Is this your son, and was he ever really blind?"

The old people realized they might get in trouble with the high priests and the rich men of the city so they simply replied:

"He is old enough to answer for himself."

The beggar was angry, and insisted that he had been blind since birth and that Jesus had miraculously restored his sight. But he was greeted with threats and ridicule. Discouraged, he sought out Jesus for comfort, recalling that Jesus had once said, "None is so blind as he who will not see."

The Raising of Lazarus

IN THE TOWN of Bethany lived Lazarus and his two sisters, Martha and Mary. They believed in Jesus, and knew that he was the Messiah sent from God. Such knowledge made all three very happy.

But, now, sad times befell the family, for Lazarus was grievously ill, and his sisters feared that he would die. Hurriedly they sent word to Jesus, who was preaching nearby.

"Come and save our brother, your friend Lazarus," they pleaded.

But, oddly enough, Jesus did not seem anxious. Instead, he continued his mission, telling his disciples that Lazarus' illness was part of God's plan.

Then one day word came of Lazarus' death. Now Jesus was determined to go to Bethany. His disciples begged him to remain where he was. Once, in Bethany, some people had thrown stones at him, because they said he had broken the Sabbath. But Jesus was not afraid.

"Our friend Lazarus is asleep, and I must wake him," he said.

The disciples were confused. They thought Lazarus was dead, not asleep. Nevertheless, they followed their Master into Bethany.

It took Jesus four days to arrive at the home of Lazarus. It was a house of sorrow. Many people had gathered to comfort Martha and Mary, the grieving sisters. When Jesus appeared, Martha ran to him.

"O Lord," she said, "if only you had come sooner, you could have saved our brother. Now he lies in his grave these last four days."

Jesus spoke comforting words.

"Lazarus will rise again," he said.

"I know," Martha replied, "he will arise on Judgment Day, in the Resurrection, for he was a righteous man. But, for now, he is gone and buried."

Jesus then proclaimed a mighty message.

"I am the Resurrection and the Life," he said. "Whosoever believes in me, *though he be dead*, he shall live again. And whosoever lives and believes in me, he shall never die."

With these words ringing in her ears, Martha led Jesus to the tomb of Lazarus. Meanwhile Mary had heard of the Master's arrival. She rushed from the house in the midst of all the mourners, seemingly joyful, for she knew the power of the Lord.

At Lazarus' tomb, the sisters knelt and wept with Jesus, who had great compassion in his heart. All those around them were struck by Jesus' devotion, and wondered could he, who had cured the lame and the blind, also raise from the dead a man buried four days in the earth?

Jesus ordered the stone rolled away from the tomb of Lazarus. Then, lifting his eyes to heaven, he cried,

"Lazarus, come forth!"

God heard Jesus' prayer, and, in a miracle surpassing all others, He restored Lazarus to life, so that the man who had been dead emerged from his tomb, still wrapped in his shroud, and stood before the astonished crowd.

Word of this mighty miracle reached the priests and rulers of Jerusalem. The most influential of these men was Caiaphas, a high priest of the Temple. He was very crafty and knew how to balance his power between the Jews and the Romans.

"If this man Jesus becomes too powerful," he said, "the Romans will get angry and cause us harm. We must rid ourselves of this so-called Messiah from Galilee."

At first, it was thought to exile Jesus. But he would not leave his country or abandon his work, for the people now joined him in greater numbers. Some openly approached him in the streets and asked to become disciples.

"Do you know that it is hard to be a disciple of mine?" Jesus would inquire. Some agreed, but joined him. Others found the task too hard, and fell by the wayside. Jesus understood, for he was always aware of man's weaknesses.

Some Famous Parables

JESUS CONTINUED to preach his parables, using examples from everyday life. He told the story of *The Missing Coin.*

Once, he said, there was a woman who had ten silver coins. By accident, one of them rolled off the table to the floor. The woman was determined to find that coin, so she lit her candle and began searching in every corner of the room. When she found the missing piece, she was so overjoyed that she threw open the windows and called to her neighbors:

"Rejoice with me, for I have found the coin I lost."

In this same way, said Jesus, God rejoices when even one lost sinner repents.

Another story had the same message. It was the *Parable of the Prodigal Son.* Once there were two brothers who lived at home with their father. The younger was im-

patient and restless. He wanted to see the world and enjoy the life of the big cities outside. Accordingly, he asked his father to give him his share of his inheritance, so that he might venture forth into the world.

The father did as his youngest son asked; and the boy went off to the city. There he gambled and lived a riotous life, until he was without money and friends. Then a famine came upon the land. Poor, disgraced, and hopeless, the young man made his way back home. It was his plan to become a servant in his father's house, so that he might pay off his debts and make himself worthy once again.

As he approached the house, his father saw him and ran to greet him joyously.

"But, father," said the prodigal son, "I am not worthy of your forgiveness, for I have sinned."

The father would hear no more. He ordered the finest robes brought from the house and a fattened calf killed for a feast in celebration of his son's return. The older brother became angry.

"I have been faithful and steadfast," he said to his father, "but with no reward. My

brother, however, wasted your money and disgraced himself. You never had a party for me, but you kill a fattened calf and prepare a feast for him."

The father replied with wisdom.

"I do not love you less than your brother," he said, "but it is fitting that we should make merry and be glad; for your brother was as good as dead, but now he is alive again. He was lost, and now he is found."

Some of Jesus' parables concerned the Pharisees, who had set themselves against all new ideas and prophecies. In one story called *The Beggar and the Pharisee*, a poor man named Lazarus, who was too ill to work, stationed himself at the door of a rich Pharisee's home. There he lay, hoping to catch a few crumbs from the rich man's table. But he was ignored, and chased by dogs in his misery. Finally Lazarus died and went to heaven, where the angels carried him to the comfort and peace of Abraham's bosom.

In time, the rich Pharisee also died. But he did not go to heaven. Instead he fell among flames and torture, so that he lay in perpetual agony. From this wretched place, the rich man could see Lazarus, the beggar, in Abraham's bosom, and he called to him and cried;

"Help me. I am thirsty and in pain. Just dip your finger in some water so that I may wet my lips."

But the gulf between Lazarus and the rich man was too great, and the beggar could not help him. The Pharisee, realizing the error of his ways, sought to prevent his brothers and his sons from knowing a similar fate. So he cried out to Abraham:

"Send Lazarus back to earth, to warn my kinsmen of the fate that awaits them if

they remain hardhearted and cruel."

"They have the words of Moses and the prophets; let your kinsmen listen to them," said Abraham.

"They won't," said the Pharisee, "but if someone from the dead goes to them they will repent."

"If they hear not Moses and the prophets," said Abraham, "they will not be persuaded by one from the dead."

Jesus told a similar story of the *Pharisee and the Publican*. The Pharisee and a humble publican went to the Temple to pray. The Pharisee looked toward heaven and said:

"I am a righteous man, not like the others. I pray; I give money to the Temple; and I fast twice a week."

The publican standing nearby lowered his eyes and bowed his head. His prayer was quite different.

"I am a lowly sinner," he said, "and I can only pray for my forgiveness."

Jesus assured his listeners that God was much more impressed with the publican than with the Pharisee, for, as Jesus said, he who exalts himself shall be brought low, and he who humbles himself shall be exalted in the eyes of God.

Jesus told another parable about wealth and humility:

A rich young Pharisee once came to Jesus and asked:

"How may I gain eternal life?"

Jesus reminded the young man of the law and the Commandments.

"Yes," said the Pharisee. "I have obeyed the law and I follow the Commandments, but I feel that there is still something more I must do."

Jesus knew what the rich man lacked.

"Go," he said to him. "Sell all your

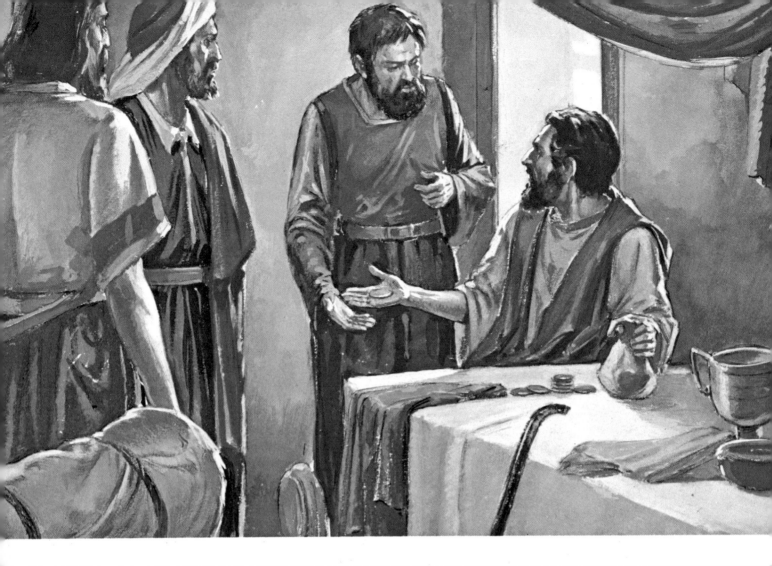

possessions and give the money to the poor. Make yourself a disciple of mine, and you shall inherit a greater treasure in heaven."

But the rich man could not bring himself to part with his worldly goods, so he went away with his head hung low. Then Jesus turned to his friends and said:

"How hard it is for a wealthy man to part with his goods. Indeed, it is easier for a camel to pass through the eye of a needle than for a rich man to enter the Kingdom of God."

The people loved to hear Jesus' parables, for they were easily understood and dealt with everyday events. For example:

A man had four servants who were very trustworthy. Because he was going on a long journey, the man divided his money among the servants and told them to take good care of it. Three of the servants took the money and invested it so that they could show a profit when their master returned. But the fourth servant was lazy, and merely buried the money in the ground. Of course, money does not grow in the ground. So, when the master returned, the clever servants were able to show a profit, but the lazy man could only hand back the same amount of money he had been given. The master was angry with this lazy man and dismissed him.

So it is, said Jesus, with the word of God. Some shall take it and use it profitably. Others will do nothing and gain nothing in the end.

Jesus considered God's teachings more important than everyday affairs. One day, he visited Martha and Mary, the sisters of Lazarus, who had been risen from the dead. They were preparing a feast to celebrate

the great event. When Jesus entered the house, Mary would not leave his side, for she was anxious to hear his teachings. Her sister Martha, however, bustled around with her pots and pans. Finally, she went up to Jesus and said:

"Lord, it isn't fair that my sister Mary sits here and doesn't help with the housework. Tell her that she must help."

But Jesus smiled. "Martha, Martha," he said, "you can do housework every day, but how often is it that I come to your home with the word of God? Mary knows this, and she will be rewarded."

Jesus told many other parables. In some of them, he compared himself to the Good Shepherd who will go any distance to save one lamb who has gone astray. Furthermore, said Jesus, the Good Shepherd is willing to lay down his life to save his sheep. This, too, Jesus was prepared to do.

Jesus Prepares to Visit Jerusalem

SINCE THE PASSOVER FEAST was soon to be celebrated, Jesus and his disciples made plans to visit Jerusalem, so that they might worship in the Temple. In his heart, Jesus knew that he would die in Jerusalem, as the prophets had predicted. But his destiny was meant to be fulfilled; and he approached the final journey with great serenity.

While passing through Samaria, on the way to Jerusalem, Jesus continued preaching and healing. At one village, ten unfortunate lepers waited at the crossroads, hoping to be healed. When they saw Jesus they rushed forward and fell on their knees. The crowd drew back, for leprosy was considered to be contagious. But Jesus knew no fear. He lifted his hands over the lepers' heads, and they were healed. Only one of the

cured men remained kneeling in thanks. Jesus was very pleased, for this man was a Samaritan, not a Jew. Now, even the Samaritans believed in Jesus and his miracles.

While passing through the town of Jericho, Jesus once again proved that all men might gain salvation, even unpopular tax collectors.

Zaccheus was the richest man in Jericho—and the chief tax collector. He was a small, unattractive person, neither better nor worse than anybody else. He was also a determined man. When he heard that Jesus, the famous prophet, was coming to town, he wanted to catch a glimpse of him. Eagerly he left his money bags and rushed out into the crowd. But, being small, Zaccheus couldn't see a thing. So he climbed a sycamore tree and sat there right over the place where Jesus passed.

"Make haste, Zaccheus," called Jesus, seeing the man in the tree, "I will stay at your house while I am in Jericho."

Everyone was surprised to see Jesus enter the home of the tiny tax collector. But Zaccheus was overjoyed. To celebrate his salvation, he gave half his money to the poor and became a devoted follower of Jesus.

After Jericho, Jesus passed through Bethany, his last stop before entering Jerusalem. There, in Bethany, he visited Martha and Mary and their brother Lazarus, who had been raised from the dead. It was the Saturday before the feast of Passover. For the next few days, Jesus would pass from triumph to death, and, then, to glory. The story of his last week in Jerusalem is sometimes known as the *Passion of the Lord*.

The Fate of John the Baptist

WHILE JESUS WAS PREPARING to enter Jerusalem, John the Baptist lay in chains deep in the dungeon of King Herod's palace. From the depths of his cell, he continued to preach the coming of the Lord and Saviour. Occasionally, his followers managed to get a message to him, and they told him of Jesus and his wonderful work.

King Herod feared John the Baptist, and was content to keep him in prison without

doing him further harm. But Herod's wife, Queen Herodias, was wicked and sinful. Because John had spoken against her, for she had been the wife of Herod's brother, she wished him dead.

One night, during a birthday feast for the king, Herodias introduced her beautiful daughter, Salome. King Herod was delighted, and wished the maiden to dance for him. He promised to award her anything her heart desired, even half his kingdom, if she would perform.

Salome agreed, and danced before the king and his guests. When she finished, Herod said:

"Now, tell me. What do you wish?"

Salome went to her mother, Herodias, for advice. Then she returned to Herod with a terrible request.

"Give me the head of John the Baptist on a silver platter," she demanded.

Herod was shocked. He tried to talk Salome out of her request, promising her jewels and great wealth. But Herodias' daughter insisted. Finally, the king reluctantly gave in, and the great prophet John was slain in the dungeon.

When the followers of Jesus heard this news, they were afraid for their Master, for the whole city of Jerusalem was seething with unrest. Everywhere, Roman soldiers were stationed, prepared to quell any riot that might begin because of the Baptist's death. In the Temple, the Pharisees and Sadducees, sworn enemies of Jesus, were plotting ways of doing him harm. Ever since Lazarus had been raised from the dead, they had feared Jesus' power and popularity. Thus, hatred and trouble were brewing in Jerusalem while Jesus prepared to make his entry.

But there were great expectations as well, for the humble Jews of the city looked forward to seeing the great Master from Nazareth. His reputation had spread in spite of his enemies' greatest efforts.

The Celebration of the Palms

AT A PLACE called the Mount of Olives, Jesus gathered his disciples. He told them that his visit to Jerusalem would be a time of fulfillment of all the ancient prophecies. In accordance with these prophecies, Jesus sent two of his men into the village nearby, in order to fetch a spotless white colt that had never been ridden. The prophets had said that the Messiah would one day enter Jerusalem astride a perfect white colt.

In due time, the disciples found such an animal and brought it to the Mount of Olives. There, Jesus mounted the colt and began the journey into Jerusalem. As he passed through the villages outside the city's walls, his disciples cried out:

"Behold the King that cometh in the name of the Lord!"

The Pharisees hearing this were alarmed. They feared a violent revolution that would make Jesus king, for they didn't understand the spiritual meaning of the word. Angrily, they cried to Jesus:

"Make your disciples stop all this shouting."

But Jesus replied:

"If these people are silent, then the stones will cry out—for my message must be heard."

Finally the procession approached the city gates. When Jesus beheld Jerusalem, the great city of the Jews, he began to weep silently, for he knew the destruction and sorrow that would someday befall every house and stone within. But then his heart was made glad, for the multitudes came out in throngs to greet him, laying their cloaks on

the road in his path. Many climbed trees for a better view, and others plucked palm leaves from the trees to wave at the Lord. Thus, the first Palm Sunday was celebrated in Jerusalem amid cries of "Hosanna"—which means "Salvation"—and amid great rejoicing.

At twilight, Jesus and his disciples returned on foot to Bethany. The first day had ended in triumph.

The Cleansing of the Temple

ON THE DAY following his triumphal entry, Jesus returned with his disciples to Jerusalem and went directly to the Temple. In ancient times, it was the custom to erect stalls alongside the Temple's walls for the purpose of selling food and objects for the sacrifice. Gradually, many merchants moved onto the Temple grounds themselves, and conducted their business in sight of the main altar.

Money lenders and changers also set up tables in the Temple, where they conducted themselves in a generally noisy and ungodly manner. Jesus understood these outrages, but this did not soothe his anger. With a whip in his hands, he rushed into the midst of the money lenders and overturned their tables and stalls, crying:

"The House of God shall be a house of prayer, not a den of thieves!"

Hastily, the merchants and money lenders retreated, but they were not soon to forget this incident. A few days later, many of them were on hand to condemn Jesus to death.

When the defilers were out of the Temple, the poor, the lame, and the blind came before Jesus, and they were miraculously healed. The priests who watched in amazement would not admit Jesus' greatness, fearing to lose their own high status in the city. In fact, they stepped forward and challenged Jesus, demanding to know who he was and by what authority he spoke. As they were speaking, a group of children entered the Temple grounds singing:

"Hosanna to the Son of David, the Messiah."

Jesus turned to the priests and said:

"You asked who I was? Out of the mouths of babes will you hear it."

Parables and Events in the Temple

AFTER CHASING the money changers and healing the sick, Jesus continued to preach in the Temple. As a teacher, or rabbi, he was entitled to do so, even though the priests and rulers of the city challenged him and wished him away. They were very cautious about causing a riot, however. Many people had gathered in the Temple to hear Jesus, and, if the soldiers had arrested him or stoned him, hundreds would have risen to his defense. So the wicked men merely tried to make Jesus look foolish in the sight of his followers.

One of them held up a coin and asked a treacherous question.

"Since you tell us to pay homage only to God," he asked, "should we continue to pay taxes to Rome?"

Jesus knew this question was an attempt to entangle him. If he said, "Don't pay taxes to Rome," he would surely be arrested. If he seemed to be fearful of Roman authority, then he would appear cowardly and weak. With perfect control, Jesus asked the man to show him the coin. The man complied.

"Whose picture is this on the coin?" asked Jesus.

"That is Caesar," the questioner replied.

"Very well," said Jesus. "Give this to Caesar, since it is his, but give unto God the things that are God's."

Properly rebuked, the troublemakers left the Temple.

On the following day, Jesus came to preach again. This time, many Pharisees and priests assembled to challenge him and interrupt his work.

"Woe unto you, scribes and Pharisees!" he called to them. "You exalt yourselves on earth, but you will be as nothing in the Kingdom of God. Even this great city of Jerusalem will one day fall to ruin; and this Temple, by which you swear, it shall crumble again, because you have based your values on material things and not on God."

The mighty rulers of the city were angered.

"This man says he is the Saviour, the Christ," they said. "But he is just a teacher from Nazareth—and no prophets ever came from Nazareth!"

Patiently, Jesus urged the sinners to repent. There was always room at God's table for the penitent, he said. Then he told the parable of *The Wedding Guest*.

A rich man once held a feast to celebrate his son's wedding. For selfish reasons, those invited failed to come. The rich man was upset, for he had prepared much food and gone to great trouble. After a while, he called his servants and told them to remind his guests of the feast. But the wicked people killed the servants rather than leave their businesses and their other tasks. Fortunately, the king of the city heard about this crime, and sent his army to arrest the murderers.

The rich man then decided to open his doors to anyone who wished to attend the celebration, and he ordered his servants to go out into the streets and invite all those at hand. Many poor and hungry people eagerly came to the feast, first dressing in their best garments as a sign of respect. One man, however, was too eager. He did not bother to change his clothing or to cleanse himself before the meal. He was forcibly made to leave. As Jesus said: "Many are called, but few are chosen."

Jesus explained his story thus: The Kingdom of God is like the feast; it is there waiting for everyone. Some people will be foolish, and refuse God's invitation to attend. Others, humble though they might be, will accept and enjoy the bounty of heaven.

Still others will be unprepared, like the man who was not properly dressed. They will be cast out of heaven.

Another parable had a similar message. It was called *The Foolish and Wise Virgins*.

Ten young ladies were supposed to accompany a bridal party on its way to the Temple. Each girl had a small oil lamp, which was to be lit at the proper time so that the procession would appear festive and beautiful. The bridegroom was detained in arriving, so the maidens sat patiently by the side of the road awaiting him. The hour grew late, and they all fell asleep. About midnight a cry was heard: "Get ready; the bridegroom is coming!"

The girls hastily prepared themselves. But five of them suddenly discovered that they had forgotten to put oil in their lamps. Nervously, they asked their wiser friends to lend them some oil. But the others needed every drop, and advised the foolish virgins to hasten and purchase the oil they needed. Then the wise maidens lit their lamps and went forth to greet the bridal party.

The foolish girls ran all over town, seeking oil. But the hour was late, and none was to be found. Finally, when they returned to the wedding feast, the doors of the house were locked, and they could not enter.

So it is with the Kingdom of God, said Jesus. God's call may come at any moment, even while you are asleep; therefore, always be ready, or you may not be able to enter the Kingdom of Heaven.

Jesus then prophesied many strange and wonderful things that would happen in the future. He spoke until evening approached; then he prepared to leave the Temple. At the door of the building, there was the customary poor box. Jesus paused and watched as the rich men of Jerusalem dropped in large sums of money to impress their neighbors.

When they were gone, a poor widow approached the box and deposited the sum of two mites, or one penny. Jesus turned to his friends and disciples, who had been with him in the Temple, and said:

"For all the wealth of the rich, God will appreciate this poor woman's gift many times over, for the rich will never miss what they gave. But this poor woman gave all she owned."

So saying, Jesus and his friends left the Temple of Jerusalem for the very last time.

The Plot against Jesus

IT WAS WEDNESDAY of the final week. Jesus and his disciples decided to preach in the city and in the villages nearby. As they walked from Bethany, the group passed a withered fig tree. Peter was surprised. He remembered having seen that same tree standing tall and straight only the day before.

Peter soon learned that Jesus had cursed the fig tree so that it withered. On Monday, Jesus had been hungry, and when he approached the tree in order to eat some figs, he found that it was bare. Jesus did not mean to be vengeful toward a harmless fig tree. He wanted to teach his disciples a lesson.

"When the word of God comes to you and you are bare as that fig tree," said Jesus, "then you will also wither."

Peter was nonetheless amazed that the tree had withered so fast.

"Have faith," said Jesus. "Faith can move mountains and fulfill all righteous desires. There is nothing like faith in God. He will feed you when you are hungry, and give you drink when you are thirsty. All these things can be accomplished by faith."

In the evening, Jesus and his followers returned to Bethany. But one disciple was missing—unnoticed by the rest. He was Judas Iscariot, a quiet, brooding man, who had remained behind in Jerusalem to take part in a terrible plot against Jesus.

Judas Iscariot

IT WAS DARK in the city. Judas crept along the narrow streets until he found the house of Caiaphas, a high priest of the Temple and the enemy of Jesus. In Caiaphas' room, several men were planning to capture Jesus so that they might turn him over to the Roman authorities.

They had to be careful. If they arrested Jesus while he was preaching, a riot might result. Therefore, it was best to take him by surprise when he was alone. Caiaphas turned to Judas:

"When would be the best time to capture your Master?"

Judas was trembling and worried.

"First you must tell me what I will get if I betray him," he said.

"The price is thirty pieces of silver," answered Caiaphas. "Tell us when it would be best to capture your Master!"

Judas was afraid, yet he accepted the deal. He told the conspirators that Jesus frequently prayed alone in the garden of Gethsemane and that he would be an easy victim at such a time.

"I shall be nearby," Judas continued. "In case you don't recognize the Nazarene, I will go up to him and kiss him on the cheek. That will be your signal."

Caiaphas was pleased, and told Judas to return to his friends. Judas left the room thinking that the priests merely wanted to arrest Jesus. He did not know that they planned to accuse him of treason against Caesar and thereby enable the Roman authorities to nail him to a cross until he was dead. The priests and Pharisees had no power to put a man to death; that power rested with Pontius Pilate, the Roman governor of Jerusalem. But the priests did have the power to bring charges against their enemies.

Jesus knew what was about to happen. Once again, he told his followers that he would be crucified in Jerusalem, and that, three days later, he would rise from the dead, for he was Christ, the Messiah, and it was his destiny to be sacrificed. Centuries before, Moses had commanded his people to sacrifice a paschal lamb and place its blood on their doorposts, so that the Angel of Death would pass over them and they would be spared. Now, Jesus would give his life on earth, so that all mankind, believing in him as the Messiah, might be spared the hopelessness of death and be redeemed of all the sins and transgressions of the world.

The Last Supper

ON THURSDAY, the entire Jewish nation prepared to celebrate the Passover feast, which commemorated the ancient Exodus from Egypt. As religious Jews, Jesus and his disciples sought a place where they might hold the ritual supper. At first, the disciples were worried about finding such a place, but Jesus said:

"In the city, you will see a man carrying a pitcher of water. Follow him. In his house, upstairs, a room will be ready and a table set. We shall hold our supper there."

As Jesus had said, the disciples found a man carrying a pitcher of water; and he led them to a modest house, where the Passover table was set and ready. That evening, Jesus and his twelve disciples, including Judas Iscariot, came into Jerusalem for the meal.

Though it was a joyous holiday, a somber mood seemed to hang over the festivities. The disciples, remembering Jesus' prophecy that he would die in Jerusalem, were sad and concerned. Nevertheless, they gathered around the table and began talking quietly among themselves. Soon a slight argument began.

"What is wrong?" asked Jesus.

One of the men replied:

"We should like to know which of us you favor most and which one will be most highly exalted in heaven?"

Once before, the disciples had wondered about this and, at that time, Jesus had said:

"He who wishes to be first in heaven must be last on earth."

Now, as a demonstration, Jesus removed his outer cloak, filled a basin with water, and knelt down before Peter.

"Let me wash your feet," he said.

Peter was amazed. How could the Lord perform such a humble service?

"Please rise, my Lord," insisted Peter.

But Jesus explained:

"When I wash your feet, you become a part of me."

Peter reflected.

"If that is true," he said, "then wash not only my feet but also my hands and my head."

Jesus was pleased at Peter's devotion and proceeded to wash his feet and the feet of all the other disciples. Then Jesus resumed his place at the table and said,

"Now you are clean; all but one of you. For one of you will betray me."

These words fell like thunder on the ears of the disciples. Nervously, each one asked:

"Is it I, Lord?"

Jesus did not immediately reply. Instead, he dipped some bread in a bowl of herbs and vinegar and passed it to Judas Iscariot as a sign of his knowledge that Judas would betray him. The others did not seem to understand this, and they remained perplexed and uneasy. Then Jesus turned to the deceitful Iscariot and said to him:

"What you must do, go and do quickly!"

Judas immediately rose from the table and fearfully left the room. The others thought that he had been sent on an errand, since Judas often handled finances for the group. They did not question Jesus any further, nor did he tell them that Judas would betray him as part of God's great plan.

Instead, Jesus rose, lifted a piece of bread in his hand, and said:

"Take this bread, which I have blessed, and eat it, for it is my body."

Then he took a cup of wine, blessed it and said:

The Gospels of Matthew, Mark, Luke, and John　　　　　　　　　　　　　*417*

"This is my blood of the new testament, which is shed for many in the remission of sins."

The disciples knew that they were witnessing a sacred act, and they knelt, and each received a piece of bread and a sip of wine in communion with Jesus. Then he said to them:

"I will not drink wine again until I drink it with God, my Father, in Heaven."

And, as they rose, he further announced:

"A new commandment I give unto you: Love one another as I love you—and all men will know that you are my disciples."

Thus, the first Communion was performed in a modest room in Jerusalem.

The Agony in the Garden

AFTER THE MEAL, the disciples sang a hymn and went out into the streets. They headed for the Mount of Olives, where it was Jesus' habit to pray alone. As they walked, Jesus turned to Peter and said:

"When I am gone, I fear my disciples will flee."

"Not I," Peter exclaimed. "I would go to prison and even to death for my Lord."

But Jesus knew the weakness of men.

"Peter," he said, "before the cock crows twice, before the morning comes, you will deny me three times and say you never knew me."

Peter was amazed and protested. Indeed, all the disciples pledged anew their undying faith. Jesus said nothing more. He walked into the quiet garden of Gethsemane on the Mount of Olives. There he

signaled Peter, James, and John to follow him and keep guard while he prayed. Jesus felt sorrowful and uneasy. Kneeling alone in the darkness, he experienced the fear and terror common to all mankind, and he called out to God:

"Father, if it is possible that I might be spared the suffering and the pain that I know will come, let me be spared. But if I must suffer as part of Your plan, let it be done. I am ready."

And, as he prayed thus, an angel appeared above him, holding forth a cup of comfort. But Jesus knew no comfort. His agony was so great that great drops of blood fell from his face. Then he seemed to swoon. When he regained his strength, the fear and terror passed away. He rose and returned, calm and unafraid, to Peter, John, and James.

Unfortunately, the three disciples had fallen asleep while they waited for their Master.

"Could you not watch even one short hour?" Jesus asked them as they awakened.

The men were embarrassed, and tried to make excuses.

"I know," said Jesus. "The spirit was ready, but the flesh is weak."

Then he asked them to watch again while he returned to his prayers. At the same

moment, led by Judas Iscariot and the high priests of the Temple, a group of Roman soldiers entered the garden.

Quietly, their swords drawn, they stationed themselves behind trees, waiting for the signal from Judas.

The Arrest

JESUS ROSE from his prayers, ready to enact God's plan. As he turned to walk from the garden, Judas came up alongside him.

"Hail, Master," he said in a friendly voice. Then holding his torch close to Jesus, he leaned over and kissed him on the cheek. Jesus understood. Quietly, he said to Judas:

"So, you have chosen to betray me with a kiss."

No sooner had he spoken, when a dozen Roman soldiers led by a priest surrounded him, their swords in the air. Angrily, the disciples jumped to their feet and attacked the soldiers. But Jesus cried out:

"Put up your weapons, for all those who live by the sword shall die by the sword!"

One of the disciples acted hastily and slashed the ear of the priest's servant with his sword. Jesus held him back and gently touched the servant's ear, so that it was cured. The disciples, seeing this, retreated into the shadows as other soldiers and priests came to capture Jesus. Cruelly, the soldiers bound him with ropes and poked him with their spears.

"Am I a common thief," asked Jesus, "that you treat me like this? Only yesterday I preached in the Temple, and you heard me and did not attack me."

But the assailants would not listen. Hurriedly they dragged Jesus from the garden of Gethsemane amid their flickering torches and upraised spears. The fateful prophecy was about to be fulfilled.

Jesus before the Priests

WAITING IN JERUSALEM were Caiaphas, the high priest, and his father-in-law, Annas, who was also an official of the Temple. Before these men, Jesus was brought as a prisoner to answer charges.

First, Caiaphas asked Jesus about his disciples and his doctrine. Jesus answered that he had never preached secretly or maliciously.

"I spoke openly to the world and in the Temple as a good Jew," he said. "You know this, your people have seen me."

Caiaphas was not pleased with this answer. He signaled one of the soldiers to strike Jesus across the face.

"Why do you strike me?" asked Jesus quietly. "If I have spoken evil, God will strike me, not you."

Outside in the courtyard of Caiaphas' house, Peter waited nervously in the shadows. He had followed the band of soldiers that had captured Jesus, and he was anxious and afraid. While he waited some men built a fire since it was cold in the morning air. As Peter moved close to warm his hands a young woman saw him and said:

"This fellow was with the prophet Jesus who is now a prisoner."

Peter was alarmed.

"That's not so," he said. "I don't even know that man."

Another person looked up.

"Oh, yes," he said, "you were one of his followers."

"No," Peter insisted. "I never heard of Jesus before tonight."

The first girl laughed.

"Don't fool us. You are his disciple. Come on, tell us what he's like."

Peter became angry. Again he denied ever knowing Jesus or being part of his band. Then, suddenly in the distance, the cock crowed in the dawn. A cold chill ran over Peter's skin as he remembered Jesus' prophecy, *Before the cock crows, you will deny me three times.*

Horrified at his weakness and disloyalty, Peter burst into tears and rushed from the scene.

The Gospels of Matthew, Mark, Luke, and John

424

Inside Caiaphas' house, the long questioning of Jesus continued. Many witnesses were brought in to testify against the man from Nazareth. Some of them were paid to lie; others purposely misinterpreted what Jesus had said, so that it might be used against him. Throughout, Jesus made no reply.

Finally Caiaphas rose and pointing his finger at Jesus, he demanded:

"Are you Christ, the Messiah, the Son of God?"

Jesus replied very simply.

"You have spoken the truth," he said.

This was too much for the high priest. Shouting "blasphemy," he turned to his council of priests,

"You have heard this blasphemy against God," he cried. "It is a sin to call oneself the Messiah; and such a sin must be punished by death. What is your decision?"

The council dared not go against Caiaphas' wishes. Without further discussion, they condemned Jesus and ordered him taken to the Roman governor, for they had no authority to put him to death. The soldiers grabbed Jesus by the arms and took him out into the street. Once alone with him, they began to punch him and spit in his face, laughing all the while and saying:

"If you're the Messiah, tell us which of us hit you and spat in your face."

Jesus did not reply. He bowed his head in prayer as they led him away.

Watching from the shadows was Judas Iscariot, who had come to Caiaphas' house

to get his thirty pieces of silver. Now he saw Jesus being led away, bound and disgraced. He knew the Romans would put his Master to death and he said to himself:

"My God, what have I done?"

Trembling, he took the money and returned to Caiaphas.

"I have sinned and betrayed a righteous man," he cried. "Take back this blood money; I'll have no part of it."

Then Judas ran from the scene to his house where he took his own life by hanging.

The priests did not want his money, for they knew it was accursed. So they took it and purchased a plot of land owned by a potter. Here the poor and unknown of the city were buried free of charge. Today such places are known as Potter's Fields—lonely memorials to the treacherous Judas Iscariot.

The Trial before Pontius Pilate

IT WAS EARLY Friday morning. Bound and guarded, Jesus was led to the palace of Pontius Pilate, the Roman governor of Jerusalem. Many of Jesus' enemies lurked outside the palace, waiting for news of what was happening.

Pilate sat on his throne surrounded by his soldiers. Before him were the representatives of the high priests.

"What charges do you bring against this man?" asked the governor.

The priests stated their case, saying that Jesus had spoken against Caesar and that he had corrupted the people with false teachings. Pilate looked over the bill of complaints that the priests had submitted. Then he summoned Jesus before him.

"Are you the King of the Jews?" he asked.

Jesus answered very quietly.

"Yes," he said, "but my kingdom is not of this world, but of the world hereafter."

Pilate was hesitant. Assuming that the complaints were religious, not political, he turned to the priests and said:

"I find no fault in this man."

The priests were emphatic. They continued to demand action from Pilate, for the law gave them no power to put Jesus to death.

"This man has corrupted the entire nation," they said, "all the way from Galilee to Jerusalem."

When Pilate heard mention of Galilee, he decided to unburden the case on King Herod, who was responsible for order in Galilee, and he ordered Jesus taken to Herod's palace in Jerusalem.

For a long time, King Herod had been submissive to the Roman authorities. When Jesus came before him, he hardly knew what to do.

"Can you perform some miracles for me?" asked the foolish king.

Jesus was silent. Outraged by this indifference, Herod, in mockery, ordered Jesus dressed up in gaudy robes, as would befit a comic "king." But he did not want to take responsibility for Jesus' death. So he ordered:

"Send him back to Pilate, and let the Romans handle him."

And so Jesus returned to the Roman governor. He was questioned again and again. For hours, Pilate listened to the arguments of the priests, and he became bored and short-tempered.

"I will have this man whipped," he said. "Then we will release him with a warning. That should satisfy you."

But the priests would not be satisfied. Pilate had a new idea. It was the custom during Passover for one prisoner to be freed upon the people's request. Pilate thought

that the crowds would ask for Jesus, since he was not a murderer or a robber like the other prisoners. But Jesus' enemies had gathered in that crowd—all the merchants and Pharisees—and, when Pilate asked them which prisoner they wanted released, they called, "Barabbas!" although Barabbas was a common thief. While Pilate was trying to resolve his dilemma, his wife came to him. She had dreamed about Jesus and believed him innocent of all the charges made by the priests. She urged her husband to release him.

Pilate went before the crowd and asked:

"Do you want me to crucify this man just because he called himself King of the Jews? This is hardly a crime."

But the people continued to shout for the release of Barabbas. Pilate was annoyed. He had other things to do, so he took a basin of water and poured it over his hands.

"I wash my hands of this matter," he

cried to the crowd, "because I find no fault in this man."

Nevertheless, to please the mob, he freed Barabbas the robber, and had Jesus flogged. Then he ordered his soldiers to dress Jesus in an old purple robe, such as a king might have worn, and crown him with a wreath of thorns. The soldiers enjoyed this cruel sport, and they hit Jesus and spat in his face as they dressed him.

Finally Pilate brought Jesus out into the courtyard before the mob.

"Here is the man," he said. "For the last time, what shall I do with Jesus who is called Christ?"

Jesus' enemies shouted:

"Crucify him! Crucify him!"

Pilate turned to Jesus, and urged him to say something, or do something that could appease the crowd. But Jesus knew that it was his destiny to die, and he said to Pilate,

"It is not in your hands, for you have no power except the power given to you by God."

Pilate then called the priests from the crowd. Once more, he argued with them, trying to avoid responsibility for Jesus' death. But the crafty priests said:

"He has called himself a king. There is only one king and that is Caesar. Any man allowing him to live is no friend of Caesar's, as Caesar will learn."

Hearing this very meaningful threat, Pilate no longer argued. He turned to the mob and announced:

"Behold your king!"

The people shouted:

"We have no king but Caesar."

"Very well," said Pilate—and he sentenced Jesus to be crucified.

The Gospels of Matthew, Mark, Luke, and John

The Crucifixion of Jesus

BEYOND THE WALLS of Jerusalem was a spot called Golgotha. There condemned prisoners were crucified upon great wooden crosses, and their bodies tossed into a pit. To this place Jesus of Nazareth came, dragging a heavy wooden cross upon his back while Roman soldiers led the way.

By now, it was midday, and many of the poor and common people of Jerusalem were out on the streets and in the markets. They could see the sorrowful procession of prisoners, weighed down under heavy beams of wood, heading toward Golgotha. Many recognized Jesus, the kindly teacher from Galilee, and they left their work to follow, weeping to see Jesus burdened by the heavy cross, an ugly crown of thorns on

The Gospels of Matthew, Mark, Luke, and John

his head and the wounds of his whipping still fresh upon his skin. But Jesus turned to them, in his agony, and said:

"Do not weep for me, but for yourselves and your children. For, behold, evil days are coming to Jerusalem."

Then he faltered under the weight of the cross, and he fell, and lay in the gutter. The soldiers ordered a man named Simon of Cyrene to lift the cross, so that Jesus might continue his final journey. So it was that Jesus, falling and in agony, reached the pinnacle of Golgotha.

Now it was time for the cruel execution. The soldiers disrobed Jesus and flung his garments to the ground. There, others grabbed up his seamless robe and began rolling dice to see which one should claim it. All this they did as Jesus was nailed by his hands and feet to the beams of the cross. He neither struggled nor cried out. But he lifted his eyes toward Heaven, and exclaimed:

"Forgive them, Father, for they know not what they do."

Then the soldiers fastened to the topmost beam of the cross a sign that read *Jesus of Nazareth, King of the Jews*. It was meant in mockery.

Once this was done, they raised Jesus on his cross to an upright position, so that he hung most painfully above the ground by the nails in his hands and in his feet.

Below, many scornful people watched this execution, calling to Jesus,

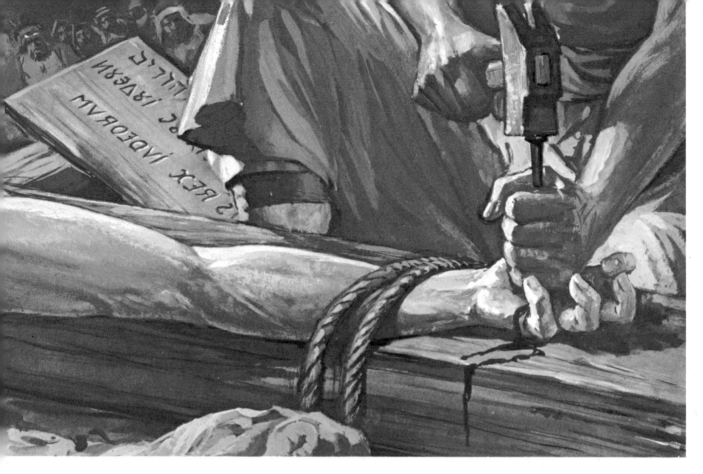

"If you are the Son of God, then save yourself and come down from the cross."

But Jesus knew his destiny. He had even refused to drink a potion that might have numbed his pain, knowing that he had to suffer for the sins of the world. And so he looked out across the city of Jerusalem in prayer, while the crowd taunted him from below.

Then he turned his eyes to the left and to the right, where two other prisoners were nailed to crosses. Both were thieves and feared death, and one of them cried to him:

"If you are the Christ, save us from this torture."

But the other said:

"If you are the Christ, remember me when you enter into Heaven." And Jesus promised to remember him.

Now, also, in the crowd at the foot of the cross, stood Mary, Jesus' mother, Mary,

436

the mother of James, and a third Mary, who was Mary Magdalene. Some of the disciples had come there as well, fearfully and in sorrow. When Jesus saw his mother and his friends, his heart was very heavy, and he whispered to the disciple John:

"Take care of my mother when I am dead."

Then a strange darkness began to fall over the city, though it was early in the afternoon; and Jesus lifted his head toward heaven, and cried in pain:

"My God, my God, why hast Thou forsaken me?"

Feeling pity, someone raised a wet sponge to Jesus' lips so that he might have some small relief. But it was too late for comfort.

"Into Thy hands I commend my spirit," cried Jesus, the man from Nazareth, and he departed his earthly life and died.

At this dark moment, the sky became pitch black. Buildings trembled, and the graveyards gave up their dead. Even the veil that hung before the Holy of Holies in the Temple suddenly tore in two, as though rent by invisible hands, and the air seemed filled with moans and crying, so that many who had scorned and mocked Jesus as he died fell on their knees and cried out:

"Truly, this was the Son of God!"

The Burial

A KINDLY JEW named Joseph of Arimathea had often heard Jesus preach and been impressed with what he had heard. This man wished to claim Jesus' body, so that he might give it decent burial.

The hour was late and the Sabbath was approaching. By Jewish law, it was forbidden to bury anyone on the Sabbath, so Joseph hurried to Pilate, the governor, to request permission to remove Jesus from the cross. At first, Pilate wished to leave Jesus there, in humiliation. But Joseph would not be dissuaded, and, finally, the Roman governor granted his wish.

Joseph then hurried to Golgotha. As he watched, a Roman centurion pierced

Jesus' side with a spear to make sure he was dead. Then they removed his body from the cross.

Carefully, Joseph wrapped Jesus in fine linen. With the aid of the sorrowing disciples, he carried the body to his home, where there was a garden. In this garden was a cave, prepared especially for burials. Here Joseph wished to bury Jesus, but, first, he called the three Marys to his side, and, together, they anointed Jesus' body with fine oils and spices. Then, with reverence and sorrow, they buried him.

In Jerusalem, the Pharisees and the priests came before Pilate and said:

"This man Jesus boasted that he would rise from the dead on the third day after his death. We must make sure that his disciples do not steal his body away and then pretend that he is risen from the grave."

"What do you want me to do?" asked Pilate.

"Place a guard at the tomb," they answered, "and roll a heavy stone before the opening, so that it is sealed. Then his disciples will be helpless, and will not be able to fool the people."

Pilate agreed, and sent three soldiers to watch at the grave, where an enormous boulder was rolled in front of the opening. Then the Sabbath came and the city was quiet. Jesus' ordeal had ended.

The Resurrection

ON SUNDAY MORNING, Mary the mother of Jesus, Mary the mother of James, and Mary Magdalene came to the garden where Jesus was buried, wishing to pay him final homage. As they approached the tomb, they saw an astounding sight. The Roman soldiers had vanished; the great boulder that had been set against the opening of the grave was now rolled away down the path; and a glorious angel, all dressed in white, sat at the entrance to the tomb.

"Fear not," said the angel to the women. "Jesus of Nazareth, whom you seek, has risen from the grave as he promised, and will shortly go to Galilee and appear before his followers."

Then the angel pointed inside the tomb where the women had seen Jesus laid to rest. Now, there was his empty shroud, and nothing more. The women were stunned. What could they believe? Had someone come and stolen Jesus' body? Mary Magdalene began to weep, and started down the path toward the city. Suddenly, she saw a shadowy figure of a man in the road.

"Why are you weeping?" asked the man.

Magdalene lowered her head to hide her tears, and she replied:

"I believe that someone has stolen the body of my Lord."

"Look at me," said the man. "Don't you know my face?"

Magdalene looked up to see Jesus standing before her, his face radiant and serene. The amazed woman reached out to touch him, for she could not believe her eyes. But Jesus withdrew, and said:

"Do not touch me now, for I have not yet ascended to Heaven."

Then he vanished.

Joyously, Magdalene ran back to the garden where Peter and John had come to behold the empty tomb. She told them what she had seen. But they were baffled and confused by her story.

In the city, word spread that Jesus of Nazareth had disappeared from his tomb and was actually risen from the dead. Many disbelieving persons said that his body had been stolen and hidden by his followers. But others believed in the resurrection, and took great encouragement from the news. Thus dawned the first Easter Sunday amid doubt and hope, for as Jesus had said earlier that week:

"Destroy this temple of my body,
and in three days I will raise it up."

The Gospels of Matthew, Mark, Luke, and John

443

Jesus at Emmaus

TWO MEN FROM THE CITY of Emmaus heard the news about Jesus' resurrection. They staunchly believed that he had risen from the dead and was the Saviour promised by the prophets of old. As they walked upon the road toward their home, they spoke of the events in Jerusalem, bemoaning the tragic death of the kindly teacher from Galilee.

As they were talking, another man, a stranger, joined them and entered into the conversation.

"What has happened?" the stranger asked.

Cleophas, one of the first two men, told the story of how Jesus had been cruelly tortured and crucified.

"But," he added, "Jesus also rose from the dead this very day, as he promised, for he was a great and wonderful prophet."

The Gospels of Matthew, Mark, Luke, and John

The stranger, seeing that Cleophas and his friend were greatly upset over Jesus' death, spoke to them with words of profound meaning.

"You must understand," he said, "that it was Jesus' destiny to suffer, according to what the prophets of old have taught us. That is why he will enter into glory."

The men from Emmaus were strongly impressed by the stranger and invited him to their home to share their evening meal.

"Abide with us," they said, "for evening fast approaches."

All three then went to the house of Cleophas. There a loaf of bread was placed before the stranger, so that he might have the honor of blessing it. This he did, and, when he raised his hands, suddenly the men saw that it was Jesus Christ, the Messiah, who had walked with them along the road and now sat at their table. As they looked on in amazement, Jesus vanished from sight.

Joyously, and in haste, Cleophas and his friends rushed back to Jerusalem to spread the word that Jesus had truly reappeared.

Jesus Appears to His Disciples

THE DISCIPLES HEARD the good news from Emmaus. They were overjoyed and yet afraid—Jerusalem had become a dangerous place for Jesus' followers. For this reason, they hid themselves in a small room in a friendly house. Here they spoke of the wonders of the resurrection.

As they talked, Jesus himself suddenly appeared in their midst and said to them: "Peace be with you."

The disciples were overwhelmed. Was this a spirit or was it really their beloved Master risen from the dead? Jesus sensed their doubts.

"Look at my hands and see the marks of the nails that pierced them," he said. "Look at my chest, where the spear was thrust. Have you not read the Scriptures that predicted these events?"

The disciples were ashamed of their doubts, and they fell down before Jesus in prayer. He blessed them and instructed them in their tasks. Then he asked for some food, and they served him broiled fish and honey.

When he had finished eating, Jesus comforted his disciples once again.

"It was necessary for me to suffer," he said, "so that I might relieve the world of sins."

Doubting Thomas

AFTER JESUS LEFT HIS DISCIPLES, Thomas came into the room. He had been out on an errand, and had missed seeing his Master. The other men excitedly told him that Jesus had actually appeared and eaten with them in that very room. Thomas would not accept their story.

"Until I can touch him with my own hands," he said, "I will not believe it."

Eight days later, the disciples were gathered in the room again, when Jesus suddenly appeared as before. Thomas was surprised, but still doubtful.

"Come forward," said Jesus. "See my hands and the place where the nail has pierced, and see on my side where I was wounded by the spear. Touch these, so that you will believe."

Thomas went over to Jesus and touched the wound on his side and the hole in each hand where a nail had pierced him on the cross. Then Thomas fell on his knees, exclaiming:

"My Lord and my God, I do believe."

Jesus pointed up a lesson from this incident:

"Thomas is blessed; he believes in me because he has seen me and touched my wounds. But more blessed are they that believe in me, even though they have not seen me."

The Ascension

AFTER MANY DAYS, the disciples returned to their homes in Galilee, and took up their old calling as fishermen. They needed time to collect their thoughts and fully appreciate the great tasks that lay ahead.

One day, they all set out in different boats to fish on the Sea of Tiberias. For hours they threw out their nets and lines, but caught nothing. Then Peter saw a man standing on the shore, and at once he recognized Jesus. Overjoyed, he leaped into the water and swam to the beach. The other disciples followed him in their boats.

It was a joyous meeting. With Jesus in their midst, the men found many fish in their nets, for he had performed a miracle as in days past. After they had eaten the fish, they gathered at Jesus' feet to hear his message.

"Go into the world," he said, "and feed my sheep—for all people are like sheep in need of a shepherd. Each one of you has his duty to spread my message and to glorify God in the name of the Father, and of the Son, and of the Holy Spirit." Then he repeated his great commandment:

"Love one another, as I love you."

For forty days, Jesus remained on earth after his resurrection. During this time he met with his disciples and continued to instruct them. One day, he asked them to meet on the Mount of Olives near Jerusalem. There he stood before them for the very last

time on earth. Then, lifting his hands in a blessing, he ascended to heaven and to God amid singing angels and great glory.

Thus ended the earthly life of Jesus, the Saviour, who, as the Lamb of God, had been sacrificed in the remission of sins for all mankind.

The Gospels of Matthew, Mark, Luke, and John

THE ACTS OF
THE APOSTLES,
AND THE
EPISTLES

Stories of the Early Christians;
Their Miracles and Hardships; of Paul, His Journeys and Letters
and His Teachings.

The Miracles and Hardships of the Early Christians

TEN DAYS after Jesus ascended to heaven, the city of Jerusalem became crowded with visitors who had come to celebrate the harvest feast of Pentecost. It was to be a supremely important day for the disciples of Jesus. They had returned to Jerusalem waiting for a sign from heaven that would mark the beginning of their mission. Once they received this sign they could go out into the world and baptize people, as John the Baptist had done, in the name of the Risen Christ. Those they baptized were later known as Christians.

At the time of Pentecost, there were only eleven disciples, because Judas Iscariot was dead. Peter had become their unofficial leader, and it was now his thought that another man be chosen to bring the number once again to twelve. An upright Jew named Matthias was selected. He and the eleven others now became known as the Apostles, or those who were to establish the new Christian faith.

Knowing that their mission was at hand, on Pentecost the apostles went to the Temple in Jerusalem. As they were in prayer, they heard the sound of a rushing wind coming from heaven. When they raised their eyes, they saw mysterious tongues of fire flickering over their heads, and they were filled with a marvelous sensation of communion with God, for the Holy Spirit had descended upon them. In addition, they experienced great intelligence and found they had received the gift of languages, whereby they could speak and understand all the foreign tongues in Jerusalem. The apostles could thus communicate with all people directly and without interpreters. They immediately began preaching the word of Christ. At first, the crowd thought that the apostles were drunk, because their voices sounded like babbling. But Peter stepped forward and announced:

"This is as the prophet Joel predicted; that all men should one day be filled with the Spirit of God; that your sons and daughters shall prophesy; and your young men shall see visions; and your old men shall dream dreams."

Then he recounted the miracle of the resurrection, and verified the report that he and the other apostles had seen Jesus risen from the dead, and announced that Jesus was God, the true Messiah. Thousands of persons in the crowd were deeply moved by this sermon, and they asked what they could do in acceptance of Christ. Peter urged them to be baptized for the remission of their sins. That day thousands became Christians in the Temple, and the Christian Church was born amid fellowship and brotherly understanding.

The healing power of Jesus had passed to his apostles, who were now filled with the Holy Spirit. One day, Peter and John came to the Temple for prayer, and walked through an arch called the Beautiful Gate. Here was stationed a crippled beggar, who was known throughout the city as the "beggar of the Beautiful Gate." When he saw the apostles, he stretched out his hand for some coins. But Peter and John had no money. Instead, Peter exclaimed:

"Look at me, and I will give you something better than money, in the name of Jesus Christ."

Then he took hold of the crippled beggar and drew him to his feet. Suddenly the man, who had been crippled since birth, found new strength in his legs, and, before long, he was leaping and jumping about and praising God at the top of his voice. Many people who knew this beggar saw the miracle, and were convinced of the powers of God. They now came to Peter to be baptized as Christians.

But the Pharisees and the Sadducees, the priests, and the other enemies of Jesus, were still set against the new religion. The high priest Caiaphas ordered Peter and John arrested. He feared the growth of Christianity, and commanded that all references to the resurrection immediately cease. But Peter was firm in his cause and would not submit. Besides, Caiaphas had heard about the beggar of the Beautiful Gate, and he knew that a miracle had taken place. Rather than excite the people by punishing Peter and John, he released them with a warning.

The two apostles returned to the Temple, where they joined their friends. As they prayed, the earth trembled beneath them, and they knew that God approved of their devotion.

As more and more people were converted to Christianity, it became necessary to establish some kind of brotherhood or community. A plan was devised whereby money would be pooled together for the common use of all Christians. Thus, a poor man could pursue his new faith without fear of going hungry. Many agreed to this plan, and sold their possessions in order to supply the fund.

A man named Ananias and his wife Sapphira were Christians who did not like this idea. They sold their possessions, but kept a good portion of the money they had received. Peter knew what they had done and questioned them, but they swore that they had deposited all their wealth in the common treasury. Because of their deceit, they both died suddenly. The others, as a result, realized the importance of honesty, and never tried to deceive the apostles.

The Sadducees and priests watched the growth of the new brotherhood with increasing alarm. They had warned Peter to cease his preaching, and yet they saw more people joining his ranks every day. Caiaphas finally ordered Peter and the apostles arrested and thrown in prison.

That night, as the apostles knelt in their cells, an angel of God appeared, and, unseen by the guards, opened all the prison gates. The apostles returned to the Temple and continued their work. When the priests came to the Temple in the morning and saw Peter preaching, they were amazed.

"Didn't we put him in prison?" they asked.

Peter stepped forth, and again announced the truth and power of Christ. But Caiaphas would hear no more. He ordered the apostles brought before the high council on charges of blasphemy. If the council found them guilty, all the apostles would be stoned to death.

Fortunately, a man named Gamaliel, a respected member of the council, rose and spoke to Caiaphas:

"We have seen many so-called messiahs appear in Jerusalem, claiming all sorts of miracles and gathering many followers to their cause. All of these groups eventually break up and disappear. I recommend that we leave these men alone. If they are false prophets, they, too, will disappear. If they are truly doing the work of God, they will survive, and we cannot fight them."

The council accepted Gamaliel's wise advice. They ordered each apostle whipped and sent away with a warning. But Peter was firm.

"We shall not heed or obey the council," he said to his friends, "for we must obey God rather than men."

As the Christian community continued to grow, dissensions arose among its members. Some persons complained that they weren't getting a fair share of the food. Others felt generally neglected. Accordingly, Peter and the apostles realized that they needed help in governing the community. They set out to find seven righteous men who would minister to the poor and hungry while the apostles preached. The men chosen were called deacons. They soon organized the community and restored harmony and order.

One of these deacons was Philip, who chose to minister to the converts of Samaria. On his way along the road from Jerusalem, Philip saw a splendid chariot drawing near. Seated in the chariot was a fine-looking Negro who had come from the country of Ethiopia, far to the south of Palestine. He wanted to know more about the Hebrew religion, and, for that reason, he was heading toward Jerusalem. To prepare himself, he had selected the Book of Isaiah to read along the way. Philip approached and asked the man if he understood the words he was reading. The Ethiopian admitted that he was puzzled about certain references to the coming Messiah made by Isaiah. Philip spent many hours telling the Ethiopian about Jesus Christ, who had fulfilled Isaiah's prophecies by his death and resurrection. The dark man was so impressed that he urged Philip to baptize him in the nearest stream, and he returned to his own land as the first Christian of Ethiopia.

One of the most noble and courageous of the deacons was Stephen, a young man totally devoted to the teachings of Jesus Christ. Because he was an eloquent speaker,

Stephen frequently lectured and debated with non-Christians about the new faith. Eventually, the Sadducees and priests heard of his work and ordered him arrested for blasphemy.

Stephen was obliged to go through the same sort of trial that Jesus had endured. He had to answer the cruel questions of the priests and stand by while false witnesses lied about his teachings. When Stephen finally had a chance to speak, he was filled with the Holy Spirit and began a sermon of such intensity and truth that the men of the council were frightened, and they covered their ears so they could not hear him.

Then, in a heavenly vision, Stephen saw Jesus standing by the side of God. The young deacon was completely unafraid and reaffirmed the glory of Christ to the angry priests. They pounced upon him, and had him dragged into the courtyard.

There, a group of burly men tied him hand and foot and began to hurl rocks at him. Stephen knelt down in pain, and called upon God to forgive his enemies and to receive his spirit into heaven. Then he collapsed under the hail of stones.

Standing nearby, watching over the garments of those men who were hurling the stones, was a Jew named Saul from the city of Tarsus. He hated the Christians and scorned the stories of Jesus Christ. Every day, he was paid to persecute Christians and send them to prison. This he did without fail, and he was greatly feared. Yet this man, later known as Paul, was to become the greatest Christian of his time.

The Conversion of Saul

SAUL HAD FINISHED his relentless work in Jerusalem; as a result, many Christians were in prison. He now wished to round up others in neighboring lands, and so he started off for the city of Damascus, in Syria.

On the road to Damascus, Saul became enveloped in a blinding light of such intensity that he could not see, and fell from his horse. Lying on the ground, he heard a faraway voice calling:

"Saul, Saul, why do you persecute me? I am Jesus; and by harming my people you harm me, as well."

Dazzled by the light and astounded by the voice of Jesus, Saul could hardly believe what was happening. Trembling with emotion, he asked:

"What shall I do, my Lord?"

Jesus instructed him to continue his journey to Damascus, but to do nothing until

he was visited by a follower of Christ named Ananias. Saul rose from the ground, still blinded from the light, and staggered toward Damascus with a fresh spirit of kindness and charity in his soul. He had become a different man.

On the street called Straight stood the house of a man named Judas. Here Saul waited, still unable to see and still dazed by his marvelous encounter on the Damascus road. Three days later, Ananias appeared at the house, just as Jesus had predicted in Saul's vision. Ananias went straight to Saul and blessed him. In that instant, Saul regained his sight. Falling to his knees, he begged Ananias to baptize him, so that he might follow Jesus Christ.

Saul now changed his name to Paul. With a new name and a new religion, he went to the synagogue of Damascus to preach the message of Jesus. The Christians of the city,

The Acts of the Apostles, and the Epistles

however, did not know of his conversion, and feared him as a powerful enemy; the Jews believed that he was a friend. When he was heard praising Christianity, all were amazed. At first, people thought that he might have lost his mind; but, as he continued to preach and practice Christianity, he became more and more hated by his former friends. One night, they conspired to kill him, But Ananias and other Christians helped Paul escape from Damascus by lowering him in a basket over the city walls.

The Conversion of Cornelius

IN THE CITY of Caesarea lived Cornelius, a Roman officer in charge of a company of soldiers. Through he did not practice the Hebrew religion, Cornelius was charitable to the poor and respected his neighbors. One day, a heavenly vision appeared to him and told him to seek out the apostle Peter who was staying in Joppa, for God was pleased with Cornelius and wished him to become a Christian.

At the same time, Peter beheld a baffling vision of birds and beasts; from this he learned that God no longer considered the old dietary laws necessary. In fact, it seemed to Peter that many of the old laws were being liberalized.

When Cornelius' messengers found Peter, they brought him to the Roman's home. Cornelius immediately fell on his knees before the apostle, and wished to worship him. But Peter raised him up, and said:

"Do not worship me; I am only a man. But let me tell you of Jesus Christ, so that you may worship him"

Outside Cornelius' house, many Christians watched as Peter and the Roman conversed. It had never been the practice to admit non-Jews into the Christian community, for most of the apostles believed that Jesus had come as a Messiah only for the Jews. But the words of God and Peter's vision of the birds and beasts seemed to point in another direction. Peter now believed that it was God's will that all men and all nations become followers of Jesus Christ, for as Peter said:

"I know God is no respecter of persons, but in every nation he who fears Him and does what is right is acceptable to Him. He sent His word to the Children of Israel, preaching peace through Jesus Christ . . . so that all may be relieved of the burden of their sins."

Then Peter baptized Cornelius the Roman, who was the first gentile to become converted. From then on, Christianity was to spread throughout the earth.

Peter Is Rescued

PETER CONTINUED to preach in small towns, bringing the word of Jesus Christ to Jew and gentile alike. News of his work reached King Herod Agrippa. Since Jesus' death, Herod had cruelly persecuted the Christians and was responsible for the death of the apostle James. Now he wanted to slay Peter, so he sent an order for his arrest. In due time, Peter was arrested and thrown in jail. To make sure that he could not escape, he was chained to two soldiers, while other men stood guard outside the door of his cell.

At midnight the soldiers fell asleep, and at the same moment an angel descended into the cell and quietly broke the chains that held Peter a prisoner. Then the angel beckoned Peter to follow him out of the dungeon. At first Peter thought that he was dreaming, but he soon found himself safely outside the prison walls and on the road to town. He hurried along and came to the apostles' house, where he anxiously knocked on the door. A servant girl answered, and was amazed to see Peter, who, she thought, had been killed by Herod. Joyously, she went to tell the apostles, but they were doubtful.

"You must have seen his ghost," they said.

Peter couldn't wait. He strode into the room and stood before his astonished friends.

"I want you to see this proof of God's deliverance," he said. Then he hastened away to hide from Herod's soldiers.

In the morning, Peter's escape was discovered. Herod blamed the soldiers, and put them all to death. He was angry, indeed. Soon after, he attended a banquet, dressed in his finest array. Suddenly, while he was making a speech, he slumped in his throne and died. After this, the apostles were not persecuted so bitterly.

Paul's First Mission

BACK IN JERUSALEM, the apostles decided to send Barnabas to the city of Antioch in Syria. A large Christian community had developed there, and the people had waited many years to hear from their leaders.

Barnabas arrived in Antioch, and was delighted to see the great number of believers assembled to greet him. For days, he preached, and talked to his friends, but, after awhile, he found the work too much for him. He then sent a message to Jerusalem requesting that Paul of Tarsus be allowed to assist him. The apostles were a bit suspicious of Paul, for they still wondered about his sudden conversion. Barnabas, however, believed in him, and journeyed to Tarsus to see him and ask for his help. Paul was enthusiastic. God had spoken to him and urged him to preach among the gentiles. Now he would have his chance. Together with Barnabas, Paul journeyed to Antioch and, for a whole year, the two men preached the gospel and encouraged the believers.

A prophet in Antioch predicted that a famine was coming. Accordingly, Paul and Barnabas arranged to collect food and water well in advance of a drought or bad harvest. Then, when lean days came upon the land, they were able to feed the hungry. When the people of Antioch were fed and out of danger, Paul and Barnabas took the extra supplies to Jerusalem. The missionaries stayed a short time in Jerusalem, and then prepared to return to Antioch. A young man named Mark, a nephew of Barnabas, asked to join them, so that he might preach the gospel. Paul and Barnabas eagerly accepted the young man's aid.

After another stay in Antioch, the missionaries felt the urge to go beyond and preach to the people of distant cities. They journeyed to the island of Cyprus, which was part of the great Roman Empire and was ruled by a Roman governor. When the governor heard about Paul and his work, he ordered the missionaries brought before him. Doubtful at first, the governor questioned Paul about the new religion. Paul spoke eloquently and convincingly, and softened the governor's heart. But a scheming magician in the court, an enemy of Christians, began to argue against the teachings of Jesus. Paul was enraged:

"You enemy of righteousness!" he exclaimed. "The Lord will strike you blind until you repent."

In that instant the magician lost his sight. The Roman governor was so amazed that he became converted on the spot, and established a Christian church in his city.

Paul and Barnabas left Cyprus and traveled through Asia Minor, the area that we know today as Turkey. At first, the Jews of that land listened to them courteously, and many accepted the teachings of Christ. But, soon, the religious leaders of the city became jealous and ridiculed the Christians. As a result, the Jews stayed away from the missionaries. In their place, many gentiles gathered at the feet of Paul and Barnabas to hear the story of Jesus.

Soon, the whole city was talking about the strange missionaries and their wonderful message. But the Jewish leaders decided to punish Paul and Barnabas for preaching blasphemy, for they did not believe the story of Jesus' resurrection. They ordered the two Christians to leave their land.

Paul and Barnabas next journeyed to Iconium, nearby. Here, again, they preached and won over many converts. Here, again, the local religious leaders were angry and took action against them. This time, their lives were threatened; and they had to flee to the town of Lystra.

A strange thing happened in Lystra. In this city, the people worshiped idols, for they had never heard of the one true God. Nevertheless, they gathered to see Paul and Barnabas speak of Jesus and his miracles. A poor cripple was in the crowd. When he heard of the wonderful healing powers of Christ, he begged Paul to cure him.

"Stand up on your feet," said Paul.

To everyone's amazement, the cripple rose and began to walk.

"These men are surely gods," said the people of Lystra. "They have come from heaven, as our forefathers promised."

Eagerly, the entire village turned out with gifts and sacrifices for Paul and Barnabas.

"You are Mercury and Jupiter," cried the people of Lystra, referring to the ancient gods of Rome; and they bowed down before the two Christians.

Paul and Barnabas were horrified. They were not gods and did not want to be worshiped. Calling for silence, they insisted that the one true God of all the world was alone responsible for life and death, for sunshine and rain, and for all the many wonders of life. Then the Christians spoke of Jesus Christ, who had brought God's message so forcefully to earth. Many of the idol worshipers were converted. Others still wondered about Paul and Barnabas.

A short time later, troublemakers from Iconium came to Lystra and spread rumors about the evil doings of the Christians. Many of the idol worshipers who had been puzzled by Paul and Barnabas now became angry and vicious. They found Paul preaching in a secluded spot, and immediately began to hurl stones at him. He fell under the crushing blows and appeared to be dead.

That night, however, he miraculously revived and dragged his aching body to the seaport, where he set sail for the city of Derbe. Again, he and Barnabas preached the word of Jesus Christ. From Derbe they went to other cities of the Middle East, and finally returned to Antioch, in Syria, where they were greeted by their fellow Christians.

The first disciples of Jesus Christ had all been Jews brought up in the Laws of Moses. When they began to preach the word of their Master, they converted other Jews to the new faith. They remembered that Jesus, as a devout Jew, had said, "I come to fulfill the Laws of Moses, not to change them."

Now, many gentiles, or non-Jews, were being converted to Christianity and certain early leaders of the new faith thought that it was wrong to accept them. They sent messengers to Antioch, where Paul and Barnabas were staying. These two missionaries, because they had converted many gentiles, were told to return to Jerusalem for a conference on whether or not gentiles would be admitted to the new religion.

Great tension existed in Jerusalem among the Christians over this matter, for many were opposed to allowing non-Jews into their community. After much debate, the aged apostle Peter rose and said:

"God urged me to preach to the gentiles, and I converted Cornelius, a Roman. I found the gentiles eager for the word of Jesus Christ and greatly receptive to his message. Therefore, let us not set up a barrier between man and God at the risk of man's salvation."

The apostle James the Less spoke along the same lines, saying:

"As long as the gentiles are pure in heart and fully accept the one true God, why should we deny them the teachings of our Lord Jesus Christ?"

These arguments were convincing. The leaders in Jerusalem decided to allow non-Jews into the Church, and sent a message to the city of Antioch confirming their decision. Paul and Barnabas, with two other men, Judas and Silas, returned to Antioch with the news. Thenceforth, all men who were pure in heart and believed in the one true God could become faithful Christians.

Paul's Second Mission

PAUL WAS EAGER to set out again on his missionary work. He approached Barnabas, and said:

"Let us revisit all the places where we have been in order to see what our fellow Christians are doing."

Barnabas agreed, and summoned his nephew Mark to join them. Paul was not pleased with Mark. Earlier, on their mission to Asia Minor, Mark had left their company and suddenly returned to Antioch. Paul decided that Mark was too inexperienced for the second mission, and told Barnabas, who became very upset. Rather than leave his nephew behind, Barnabas took Mark on his trip to Cyprus, while Paul went back to Asia Minor. Because of this matter, the two great missionaries did not part on the most friendly terms.

Paul chose Silas to accompany him to Syria and to the familiar cities of Lystra and Derbe. In Lystra, he learned about the work of a young Christian named Timothy, who had a gentile father and a Jewish mother. When Paul met young Timothy, he was so impressed with his intelligence and devotion that he asked him to join the missionary expedition.

For months, the three Christians preached and established the foundations of their new religion. They finally reached the seaport of Troas, which was located near present-day Istanbul. When Paul finished his work at Troas, he first thought of returning eastward, back toward Antioch. But, one night, as he slept, he had a vision in which a man from a more distant country called Macedonia urged him to "come over and preach to us."

Paul was convinced that this was a message from God urging him to expand his missionary work into the western part of the world, which we know as Europe today.

The next morning, Paul advised Silas and Timothy that they would embark for Macedonia, and the city of Philippi. In those days, this vast area belonged to Rome, and the people there worshiped many gods. Nevertheless, there were a few Jews in the land, as well as many gentiles hungry for a new faith and a new salvation.

Paul sought out the Jewish community in Philippi and found that the people met for their prayers on the Sabbath by the river bank. He joined them, and, afterward,

spoke of Jesus and his teachings. In the group was a wealthy lady named Lydia. She was deeply moved by Paul's words and asked to be baptized there at the river, along with her servants. Then she invited the missionaries to stay at her home while they were in Philippi. By this time, a young doctor named Luke had joined Paul and his friends. Luke was a gentile who believed in Jesus Christ. He kept faithful records of all the things that Paul said and, eventually, he wrote one of the most important Gospels.

In Philippi there was a man whose servant girl was gifted in telling fortunes. The girl herself was not aware of her powers, for she had been possessed by an evil spirit. Every day, she fell into a trance, speaking the words of the evil spirit, while her master collected money for the fortunes that she told.

Paul and Silas used to pass the house where the fortune teller lived. Every time she saw them, she cried out:

"Behold the men of God, who have come to bring us salvation!"

Paul knew that the girl was possessed, and wished to cure her. Approaching the place where she was, he cried:

"In the name of Jesus Christ I command the evil spirits to leave you!"

In that same hour, the girl was restored to her right mind and she was at peace; however, she could no longer tell fortunes. Her greedy master was enraged. When he was told that Paul and Silas had cured the girl, he called the Roman soldiers and had them arrested.

By this time Paul and Silas were well known in Philippi, and they had many enemies. The Romans, knowing this, ordered them to be severely beaten and thrown into prison. This was done. Paul and Silas were placed in stocks, fastened by their hands and feet, and left alone in a dark, dirty cell.

At midnight, the two missionaries heard a fearsome rumbling in the earth, and, suddenly, all the doors of the prison swung open and all the stocks and chains fell apart. The prisoners, including Paul and Silas, were overjoyed, but a young Philippian jailer was fearful for his life. How could be explain this miracle and not be charged with treason? He was so alarmed that he decided to kill himself rather than face disgrace. Paul leaped to his side and held his sword.

"Do not kill yourself!" he cried. "We will not run away!"

True to his words, not one of the prisoners left his cell, even though the doors were opened. The jailer realized that he was in the presence of holy men, and fell at their feet, crying:

"How may I be saved?"

Paul then spoke of Jesus Christ, and won over the jailer to Christianity. In the morning, the jailer spoke to his friends and to the Roman officials. He described the wonderful teachings of Paul and Silas and how they had been kind to him.

The two missionaries were fed and told that they were free. But, oddly enough,

Paul would not go. He demanded an audience with one of the Roman judges.

"I have a serious complaint," said Paul. "I am a Roman citizen, like you, and yet I was dragged through the streets, beaten, and put into jail without a trial."

The judge was afraid. He knew that Paul was right and that the officials of Philippi had acted hastily. He apologized, and begged Paul to leave peacefully, if not for his sake, then for the sake of the young jailer who had been converted the night before. Paul knew that he had made his point and, with Silas, he left Philippi.

The missionaries continued to preach throughout Macedonia. From Thessalonica to Berea, their message was heard in many cities. Often they were attacked. Riots flared up against them. Many believed; others scoffed. Danger and success went hand in hand for the missionaries; but they were undaunted. At last, Paul decided to enter the ancient land of Greece, and he summoned Timothy and Silas to join him.

The most beautiful city in Greece was Athens. Not only was Athens an important center of business, science, and religion, it was also adorned with the noblest buildings and sculpture to be seen anywhere in the world. Paul could not help but be impressed by the city and especially by the Acropolis, a mighty hill, crowded with many temples and statues, that overlooked the ancient city.

Though Paul found Athens nobly beautiful, he was distressed by the idol worship there. No one spoke of the one true God or of Jesus Christ. Instead, they paid homage to statues representing warriors, hunters, and supernatural beings. There was even one monument built to the "Unknown God." This intrigued Paul. At least, he said to himself, the Athenians were aware of the possibility that a greater God did exist.

In order to preach to the widest audience he could find, Paul went to the Hill of Ares in the center of the city. Here, learned men and philosophers met every day to exchange ideas. Everyone was interested in what Paul had to say; and at first he was given a courteous hearing.

"I have seen your altar to the 'Unknown God,' " he said. "I declare to you that this is the one true God who made all the heavens and earth and who sent us His only son, Jesus Christ. I also tell you that Jesus Christ suffered and died for our sins, and that he was resurrected from the dead so that he might sit in judgment of all men upon the appointed day of reckoning."

The mention of Jesus' resurrection was apparently too much for the Athenians, and they began to laugh. Worldly-wise as they were, however, they left Paul in peace and told him to come again, next year, and speak of his "Unknown God." Then they went about their business as usual. One man named Dionysius did believe what Paul said. He and a few others became Christians that day in Athens.

From Athens Paul journeyed to Corinth, another Greek city. Here he stayed with some Jewish friends and helped them at their business of sewing canvas for tents. Paul had been trained as a boy in this trade. On Sabbath, he went with the Jews to the synagogue and spoke of Jesus and the new faith. Timothy and Silas joined him in Corinth. All three vigorously preached the new testament, but the Jews were unreceptive. This angered Paul.

"From now on I will speak only to the gentiles!" he exclaimed.

A few Jews did convert to Christianity, and held secret services in their homes. After a year, this practice spread, and began to alarm the enemies of Christ. When the new faith seemed to be getting out of hand, the religious leaders of Corinth arrested Paul and his colleagues and brought them before Gallio, the civil ruler of the city. Gallio listened to the complaints of Paul's enemies and was annoyed.

"Don't bring me your religious problems," he said. "I am here to deal with civil matters and not with God."

He then dismissed the case and retired, without putting an end to the fighting and disputes. Paul continued to preach in Corinth, but, with Passover approaching, he decided to return to Jerusalem for the great religious festival. After a brief rest in the Holy City, Paul was off on his mission again, this time returning to Antioch.

In the city of Ephesus, across the water from Athens, most people worshiped the goddess Diana. There was, however, a synagogue for the Jews, who believed in the one true God and who read the Holy Scriptures of Moses. One of these Jews, named Apollos, had learned about John the Baptist and his concept of a new religion. Apollos had accepted these ideas and baptized many of his friends. However, neither he nor his followers had ever heard of Jesus Christ or knew the events of his life and death.

One day, some Christians came to Ephesus and were told about Apollos and his group. They sought him out and asked:

"Have you never heard of Jesus Christ and the Holy Spirit?"

Apollos confessed his ignorance, but was eager to learn. He soon realized that what he had established was only a part of the religion of Christ; and he hastened to inform his followers of the great news. After this, the Christian faith began to take form in Ephesus.

When Paul arrived in the city, there were many persons ready to accept the new religion. He taught and preached for months. He also performed many miracles of healing, so that his fame spread far and wide. Every day, countless numbers of the sick and infirm came to be cured. When the people of Ephesus saw the power of God, many repented their old ways. They burned their books of black magic and accepted the teachings of Christ.

But not all the Ephesians were sympathetic to Jesus. The greater number of them still worshiped the goddess Diana and, every day, they bowed down before tiny silver statues made in her image.

Demetrius was the leading silversmith of Ephesus who fashioned the idols of Diana. He became worried that the increasing number of converts to Christianity would ruin his business, so he called together many other silversmiths of the city and said:

"We earn our money by making idols of the goddess Diana. Now this man Paul comes along and says that such idols are false and that the one true God needs no idols. If this keeps up, we shall all be paupers."

Demetrius' argument was very convincing, and his colleagues joined him in an attempt to discredit Paul. They marched up and down the streets of the city crying:

"Great is Diana, the goddess of Ephesus!"

Some of Paul's followers heard this cry and came out to investigate. When the silversmiths saw them, they attacked them, and there was a great riot in the streets. Paul tried to help his friends, but was prevented by other Christians who knew that the angry mob would tear him to pieces. By nightfall, the riot still continued and many were hurt. Finally, a high city official came upon the scene and demanded silence.

"People of Ephesus," he cried, "by such a commotion you bring discredit upon the great goddess Diana. The men whom you have attacked are not robbers or criminals. If the silversmiths have a complaint against them, let them go to a court of law. Remember! We have the good reputation of our city to consider."

The Ephesians were convinced by this appeal to reason, and released the Christians. Nevertheless, a few Ephesians lay in wait for Paul, who was supposed to board a ship that night for Syria. Fortunately, Paul learned of the plot. He escaped and set sail for Macedonia instead.

For many months, Paul traveled the familiar route of his mission; from Macedonia back to Asia Minor and the cities of Derbe and Troas. As always, he preached and made new converts to Christianity. More important, he enriched the faith of those already following the ways of Christ, often solving difficult problems faced by the young churches.

At last, Paul decided to return to Jerusalem, the center of all religion. He knew that danger awaited him there, and, each time he met with old friends along his route, he made a special effort to bid them good-by and to leave them with a memorable message.

One day, when he was boarding a ship for the long journey back to Palestine, a multitude of the faithful followed him to the shore. They warned him of the dangers ahead and prayed for a last message. Paul raised his hands and said:

"The best thought that I can leave you is very simple. As our Lord has said, it is more blessed to give than to receive. Remember this, and be kind to the weak and suffering."

Then Paul set sail along the route to Palestine, touching the ancient ports at Cyprus, in Syria and, finally, Caesarea—the last stop before Jerusalem.

Paul's First Trial and Escape

WHEN THE JEWS of Jerusalem heard that Paul returned, they became enraged.

"This is the man who has gone around the world trying to destroy the Jewish faith," they cried. "He has even allowed non-Jews into the synagogues, and he must be punished."

Paul's friends heard these accusations, and urged him to prove his good intentions by going to the great Temple and worshiping in the manner of a faithful Jew. Paul agreed. He went to the Temple, and performed the rites of purification according to the Laws of Moses.

On the streets, near the Temple, were some of Paul's most relentless enemies. When they saw him, they began to rouse the crowd:

"There he is! There is the man who is trying to bring down the Temple and destroy the faith!"

Paul had entered the Temple alone, but he was accompanied to the door by two friends from Greece. The angry Jews thought that he had defiled the Temple by allowing these strangers inside, so they rushed upon Paul and dragged him into the streets.

A great riot followed instigated by angry and dissident men. Fortunately, a band of Roman soldiers heard the commotion. They rescued Paul and allowed him to climb to the highest stair of the Temple. There, speaking in Hebrew, Paul told the crowd the story of his life, from the time when he persecuted Christians to his great revelation of Christ on the road to Damascus. Paul also described his missionary work and kept repeating the fact that he had always been a good Jew and that the work that he was doing in the name of Jesus was in accordance with Jewish prophecy. The crowd listened patiently. But when Paul spoke of converting the gentiles, they became enraged again, alarming the Roman authorities, who bound Paul and led him away to be flogged. When he was brought before the judge, Paul asserted his independence as a Roman citizen and demanded a fair trial. The judge was cautious. He ordered that Paul be turned over to the Jewish priests.

During the trial, Paul noted that the two great factions of Jewish rule, the Pharisees and the Sadducees, were assembled. In order to cause dissension among them, he cried out:

"Listen to me, I am a Pharisee and I believe in the resurrection of the dead."

The Sadducees did not believe in resurrection. They immediately began to call for Paul's execution, while the Pharisees, taking him for one of their own, loudly advocated his freedom. The Romans, seeing the futility of this trial, brought Paul back to the prison.

Though Paul was locked up in a cell, his enemies were determined to kill him. Forty of them took a pledge that they would not eat a bite of food until Paul lay dead at their feet. Then they began to plot a way to kidnap the Christian as he was led from the prison to the courtroom.

Paul's young nephew overheard the plotting and sent a warning to his uncle. Once again, Paul used the fact of his Roman citizenship as a means of salvation. Calling upon the prison commandant, he described the plot against his life.

"In order to save me," said Paul, "I recommend that several hundred soldiers take me to Caesarea and the Roman governor, Felix. This way I will be out of your authority and saved from my enemies."

The commandant agreed and wrote to Felix, asserting Paul's innocence and bidding him protect Paul as a Roman citizen.

That night several bands of soldiers entered the prison courtyard. They wrapped Paul in a cloak, placed him on a horse in their midst, then galloped away toward Caesarea. Paul's enemies were hardly aware of what was happening.

The next day the apostle was put in the prison of Caesarea to await a trial. He knew that he was now on the road to Rome, and that it would be his mission to preach in the great capital of the world, where many waited for the Gospel.

The Trials before Felix and Festus

A FEW DAYS after his arrival, Paul was conducted to the throne room of Felix, the Roman governor in Caesarea, for still another trial. This time, Paul's enemies sent Tertullus, a skillful lawyer, to prosecute on their behalf in Caesarea.

Tertullus rose before Felix and bowed with a flourish.

"O mighty Felix," he said, "you are a great and noble ruler who has brought us all prosperity and peace. Every one of us owes you a debt of thankfulness."

Felix knew that this flattery was only meant to prejudice his judgment, so he urged Tertullus to get to the point. The lawyer from Jerusalem immediately changed his tone and began to lash out against Paul, describing him as a ringleader of the Nazarenes, a rabble-rouser and blasphemer! He then called for the severest possible punishment.

Felix now instructed Paul to defend himself. Once again the dauntless apostle of Christ rose and spoke of his work, his mission, and his honorable purpose. The Roman governor was perplexed. He realized that Paul was innocent, but he also wanted to appease the Jews, so he ordered Paul returned to prison pending further evidence.

For two years, Felix kept Paul in prison, allowing him many privileges. At times, he even brought Paul into his private chambers, so that he might hear more about Christ and the new testament. On one such occasion, Felix became overwhelmed by his troubled conscience and his many sins. Trembling, he sent Paul back to his cell. He secretly hoped that someone would offer him a bribe for the prisoner's escape. But no one did.

After a time, a new governor named Festus replaced Felix in Caesaera. Festus was very serious about his job, and journeyed to Jerusalem in order to learn more about the Jewish people over whom he ruled. In Jerusalem, Paul's enemies appeared before Festus and urged him to release Paul in their custody. They intended to kill him.

Festus was very cautious. He advised the Jews that he would return to Caesarea and investigate the case. In ten days, he said, they could come there for another trial.

Ten days later, Paul stood before his accusers. Once more, he firmly asserted his innocence and described his noble work. Festus was perplexed, as Felix had been. He dismissed the council and turned to Paul.

"Let me send you back to Jerusalem," he said. "I am sure you will receive a fair trial."

Paul knew differently.

"I shall not go to Jerusalem," he exclaimed, "but rather to Rome. I appeal to Caesar himself—as is my right under Roman law. If he finds me guilty, then I will accept my punishment."

Festus, not wishing to pass judgment on Paul himself, was relieved.

"You have appealed to Caesar," he said. "To Caesar you shall go."

A few days later Festus entertained a royal visitor, King Agrippa of nearby Jordan. While the two men were dining, Festus related the story of Paul, the prisoner, who had caused so much debate and dissension. King Agrippa was anxious to see Paul for himself.

The next day, Paul was led into the throne room of Festus, where he found a large crowd assembled. There was the Roman governor with King Agrippa and the king's sister Bernice. Agrippa ordered Paul to tell his story.

Once again, the apostle began the story of his life, from the time of his revelation on the road to Damascus to the days of his missionary work among Jews and gentiles alike. Paul also spoke eloquently of Jesus Christ—his life, his death, and his resurrection, and he preached the path to salvation through belief in the resurrected Lord. King Agrippa was deeply moved and said:

"You almost persuade me to become a Christian."

Paul was honored.

"I wish you would become a follower of Christ," he replied. "I wish all men could hear my message."

But Festus was not as easily moved.

"Too much learning has made you crazy," he said to Paul, and he ordered him taken back to the cell.

Agrippa then turned to Festus and shook his head.

"It is too bad," he said. "This man seems innocent enough, and he could go free. *But* he has appealed to Caesar, and to Caesar he must go."

The Acts of the Apostles, and the Epistles

The Great Shipwreck

PAUL WAS SENT to Rome in chains, under the care of Julius, a Roman centurion. With several other prisoners and passengers, Paul set sail on a cargo ship bound for Italy. Luke, the physician, accompanied Paul and kept a diary of the fearsome journey that followed. This is what he wrote:

"We set sail from Caesarea amid many well-wishers who had come to bid farewell to Paul. At the port of Sidon, we were allowed to go ashore briefly to visit some Christians there, for Paul had become friendly with Julius, our captain. At the seaport of Myra we made our last stop. There, we boarded a larger ship, loaded with grain and other cargo. Then we headed out into the vast Mediterranean Sea.

"At first all seemed well, but soon dark clouds arose in the heavens and the seas became choppy and fierce. Paul went on deck and told the captain that much injury and damage would follow if we continued. So the ship was steered to a small harbor, called Fair Havens, on the island of Crete. Shortly after, the captain was anxious to continue the journey, in spite of Paul's warnings, and as the storm had somewhat abated, he set sail once more—venturing far out onto the sea. This time, a great gale arose, and the sky was black, day and night, for weeks. We could not go forward and we could not turn back, so we foundered in the waves, helplessly. The captain was alarmed. Rather than see us all drown, he ordered much of the cargo tossed overboard, to lighten the ship. This helped little, and the storm continued to rage, causing the passengers to be afraid. Only Paul was courageous. He appeared and told us of a dream in which God promised that no one would be lost in the storm, since it was destined that Paul reach Rome.

"For two weeks, we rocked back and forth on the waves, and then someone sighted land far off in the mist. A few of the sailors were too anxious to get off the ship. Secretly, they headed toward the lifeboats in order to get away. But Paul saw this, and warned the captain that God wanted all the crew and passengers to remain aboard. So the captain cut the lines of the lifeboats, and they floated away without anyone in them. The people then demanded food, for they had been fasting in order to conserve our meagre supply. Paul said we might eat and thank God for our safety. When we had eaten enough, we tossed the remaining supplies overboard to lighten the ship.

"By now, the ship had floated close to land, and we could see a rocky harbor nearby. The mainsail was raised, the rudder loosened, and many anchors dropped so that we could climb off the ship and swim ashore. But then, the prow hit a rock and the entire vessel began to split apart. Even so, not one passenger drowned or was lost.

We all swam safely to the island of Melita, where the inhabitants welcomed us and built fires for our comfort. Thus, we survived a terrible sea voyage, and Paul was at last on his way to Rome."

Paul's Last Journey

ON THE ISLAND of Melita, or Malta, Paul, Luke and the others rested for three months. The islanders at first thought Paul was a common prisoner, for they saw his chains and heard many wicked rumors about him. Then, one day, while Paul was carrying wood to a fire, a poisonous snake bit his hand. The people surely thought he would die because he was a wicked man. Instead, nothing happened at all, and Paul went about his work. Now the islanders knew that Paul was favored by God, and they respected him.

On that same island lived Publius, a chieftain, who invited Paul to his home, where Publius' old father lay ill and dying of a fever. But Paul prayed for him and eventually he was healed. Once again, many came to believe in Paul, and, by the time he was ready to set sail again, the people of Melita had proclaimed him their friend forever, and gave him many presents as a token of their respect.

From Melita, Paul went by ship to Rome, stopping along the way at the ports of Syracuse and Puteoli. The Roman captain, Julius, was kind to his prisoner, and allowed him to visit the Christians at these places.

Finally, the ship reached the port of Rome. At last, Paul had arrived at the world's chief city where the emperor Caesar lived, surrounded by a vast population, and by luxuries unlike any in the world. In such surroundings, Paul was at first anxious and unsure. But, as he walked the roads toward the center of the city, many Christians who had heard of his coming rushed out to greet him and to cheer his heart. Paul was no longer afraid, even when he was handed over to the Roman authorities. They treated him well, gave him his own quarters, and set only one guard over him.

A few days later, Paul went before the Jewish authorities in Rome and learned, to his great surprise, that they had never received any message from their colleagues in Jerusalem about Paul or his supposed crimes. As far as they were concerned, the case was closed. Greatly relieved, Paul went about his work preaching to Jews and gentiles alike.

Paul settled in Rome in his own house, and widened his circle of friends and followers. He had one servant, a young man named Onesimus, who devoted his life to serving the great apostle. At first Paul didn't know that Onesimus was a slave who had run away from his master, Philemon. In those days a slave was the personal property of his master and he could not do as he pleased. When Paul learned this news, he wrote a letter to Philemon, begging for Onesimus' freedom—a letter so eloquent that it probably softened Philemon's heart, for he wrote:

"Perhaps Onesimus fled you for your own good, since it is better that we all look upon our fellow men as brothers, not as servants."

Paul's Great Letters

PAUL WROTE many other letters, mainly to his friends in the churches he had visited. These letters were intended to clarify many difficult points of faith and to strengthen belief and love in Jesus Christ.

The letter that he wrote to the church at Ephesus was called the *Epistle to the Ephesians*. Those he wrote to the people at Thessalonica were called the *Epistles to the Thessalonians*. Especially beautiful was one letter that he wrote to the Christians in Corinth. In this letter, the *First Epistle to the Corinthians*, the great apostle declared the glory and the beauty of spiritual love and charity. He said:

"Though I speak with the tongues of men and of angels, and have not love, I am become as sounding brass or a tinkling cymbal. And though I have the gift of prophecy, and understand all mysteries, and all knowledge; and though I have all faith, so that I could move mountains, and have not love, I am nothing . . . for love suffereth long, and is kind; love envieth not . . . but beareth all things, believeth all things, hopeth all things, endureth all things . . . and never faileth."

Paul was very old. He could look back on his life and say with honesty that he had "fought the good fight and kept the faith." Thousands and thousands of weary souls had been converted to Christianity by Paul, and he truly established the religion now known in every part of the world.

We do not know exactly what happened to Paul after his letters were written. But, in A.D. 64, the insane emperor of Rome, Nero, set fire to the city. When the conflagration had died down, he blamed the Christians for starting it and many were put to death. It is believed that Paul was executed at this time. It is also said that the aged apostle Peter died that same day, hanging on the cross, as Jesus had died—but upside down, by his own request, so that, in death, he would be lowlier than his Lord.

Thus, two of the greatest saints in all history, St. Peter and St. Paul, finished their days in Rome.

THE

REVELATION

OF

ST. JOHN

THE DIVINE

The Wonders of Future Days

ABOUT THIRTY YEARS AFTER Peter and Paul had died, an old man sat in lonely contemplation on the island of Patmos in the Aegean Sea. He had been sent there as a prisoner by the Romans, who had intensified their persecution of the Christians. This old man was John of Ephesus. There is a difference of opinion as to whether he was the John who was a disciple of Jesus, or another man who had preached the Gospel in Asia Minor.

Whoever he was, this holy man saw awesome and majestic visions during his island isolation. The Revelation, or the Apocalypse, as it is sometimes called, is John's retelling of the things he had seen in his visions. He wrote:

"I was in the spirit on the Lord's day, and heard behind me a great voice, as of a trumpet, saying 'I am Alpha and Omega, the first and the last. What you see, write in a book, and send it to the seven churches which are in Asia.'

"And I turned to see the voice that spoke to me. And I saw seven golden candlesticks; and in the midst of the seven candlesticks one like the Son of Man, clothed with a garment down to his feet and around the chest a golden girdle.

"And his countenance was as the sun shining in its strength. And when I saw him, I fell at his feet as if dead. And he laid his right hand upon me saying, 'Fear not; I am the first and the last. I am he that liveth and was dead; and behold I am alive for evermore, Amen; and have the keys of hell and of death. Write the things which thou hast seen, and the things which are, and the things which shall be.' "

John tells us of his being overwhelmed by seeing God enthroned; of seeing the destruction wrought upon the sinful cities of the earth—the Babylons; of viewing the final battle between the angels and the powers of evil, with Satan being chained for a thousand years. A memorable part of the book records the vision of the Four Horsemen of the Apocalypse setting out to devastate the earth. Pestilence rides a white horse, war rides a red horse, famine rides a black horse, and death rides a pale horse.

The Revelation of St. John the Divine

John writes of a majestic vision in which he saw the Lord on a great, white throne, surrounded by the Heavenly Host on the day of the Last Judgment.

"And I saw the dead, small and great, stand before God; and the books were opened: and another book was opened, which is the book of life. And the dead were judged by what was written in the books, according to their deeds."

In a final vision, John saw the wonders of future days. He wrote:

"And I saw a new heaven and a new earth: for the first heaven and the first earth were passed away; and there was no more sea.

"And I, John, saw the holy city, new Jerusalem, coming down from God out of heaven, prepared as a bride adorned for her husband. And I heard a great voice out of heaven saying, 'Behold, the tabernacle of God is with men, and he will dwell with them, and they shall be his people, and God himself shall be with them, and be their God. And God shall wipe away all tears from their eyes; and there shall be no more death, neither sorrow, nor crying, neither shall there be any more pain: for the former things are passed away.' And he said to me, 'It is done, I am Alpha and Omega, the beginning and the end. I will give unto him who is thirsty of the fountain of the water of life freely.'

"And one of the seven angels talked to me, saying, 'Come, I will show you the bride, the Lamb's wife!'

"And he carried me away in the spirit to a great and high mountain, and showed me that great city, the holy Jerusalem, descending out of heaven from God.

"And I saw no temple there, for the Lord God Almighty and the Lamb are its temple. And the city had no need of sun, neither of the moon, to shine in it, for the glory of God did lighten it and the Lamb is the Light thereof.

"And he showed me a pure river of water of life, clear as crystal, proceeding out of the throne of God and of the Lamb. Along the street, by the river, grew the tree of life, which bore twelve kinds of fruit, and yielded its fruit every month; and the leaves of the tree were for the healing of the nations.

"And the Lord God of the holy prophets sent his angel to show to his servants the things which must shortly be done. And he said to me, 'Behold, I come quickly. Blessed is he who follows the prophecy of this book.'

"Amen. Even so, come, Lord Jesus."

PRONOUNCING GUIDE

This list includes a modern phonetic spelling of difficult names found in the stories.

A–bed'ne–go   *uh–*BED*–nuh–go*
Ab'i–gail   AB*–ih–gale*
A–bim'e–lech   *uh–*BIM*–uh–lek*
A–bin'a–dab   *uh–*BIN*–uh–dab*
Ad–o–ni'jah   *add–uh–*NYE*–juh*
A–has–u–e'rus   *uh–haz–oo–*EE*–rus*
A–ha–zi'ah   *ay–huh–*ZYE*–uh*
A–him'e–lech   *uh–*HIM*–uh–lek*
An–a–ni'as   *an–uh–*NYE*–us*
An–ti'o–chus   *an–*TIE*–oh–kus*
An'ti–pas   AN*–tih–pass*
Ar–i–ma–the'a   *air–uh–muh–*THEE*–uh*
Ar–ta–xerx'es   *are–tuh–*ZERK*–zeez*
Ath–a–li'ah   *ath–uh–*LIE*–uh*
Ba'al   BAY*–ul*
Ba'laam   BAY*–lum*
Ba–rab'bas   *buh–*RABB*–us*
Bel–shaz'zar   *bell–*SHAZ*–er*
Ben–ha'dad   *ben–*HAY*–dad*
Be–thes'da   *beh–*THEZ*–duh*
Bo'az   BOH*–az*
Caes–a–re'a   *cess–uh–*REE*–uh*
Ca'ia–phas   KAY*–uh–fuss*
Ca'naan   KAY*–nun*
Ca–per'na–um   *kuh–*PURR*–nay–um*
Chal–de'an   *kal–*DEE*–un*
Da–ri'us   *dah–*REE*–us*
Do'eg   DOH*–eg*
E'dom   EE*–dum*
E–li–e'zer   *ee–lih–*AY*–zer*
E–li'sha   *ee–*LYE*–shuh*
Em–ma'us   *eh–*MAY*–us*
Eph'e–sus   EFF*–uh–sus*
E'phra–im   EE*–frah–yim*
Ge–ha'zi   *ghee–*HAY*–zye*
Ger'shom   GER*–shom*
Geth–sem'a–ne   *geth–*SEM*–uh–nee*
Gol'go–tha   GAHL*–goh–thuh*
Haz'a–el   HAZ*–uh–el*
Hol–o–fer'nes   *hol–oh–*FUR*–neez*

Hu'shai   HOO*–shy*
Ja–i'rus   *jay–*EYE*–rus*
Ja'pheth   JAY*–futh*
Je–ho'ram   *jee–*HO*–rum*
Je–hosh'a–phat   *jee–*HOSH*–uh–fat*
Jeph'thah   JEFF*–thuh*
Jo'ash   JOH*–ash*
Laz'a–rus   LAZ*–uh–rus*
Lyd'da   LEED*–uh*
Lys'tra   LISS*–truh*
Mac'ca–bees   MACK*–uh–beez*
Mag–da–le'ne   *mag–duh–*LEE*–nuh*
Mat–ta–thi'as   *mat–uh–*THIGH*–us*
Mel–chi'ze–dek   *mel–*KIZ*–eh–dek*
Me–phib'o–sheth   *meh–*FIB*–uh–sheth*
Me'shach   ME*–shack*
Mo–ri'ah   *muh–*RYE*–uh*
Neb–u–chad–nez'zar   *neb–uh–cud–*NEZ*–er*
Ne–he–mi'ah   *nee–heh–*MY*–uh*
Phar'i–see   FAIR*–uh–see*
Phil'ip–pi   FIL*–ip–pie*
Phi–lis'tine   *fih–*LISS*–tin*
Pi'late   PIE*–lut*
Pot'i–phar   POT*–ih–fer*
Re–ho–bo'am   *ree–hoh–*BOH*–um*
Sa–lo'me   *sa–*LOW*–may*
Sa–ma'ri–a   *suh–*MAY*–ree–uh*
Sap–phi'ra   *suh–*FIE*–ruh*
Sa'rai   SAYR*–eye*
Sen–nach'e–rib   *sen–*NACK*–uh–rib*
Sha'drach   SHA*–drack*
She'chem   SHEE*–kum*
Sis'e–ra   SIS*–uh–ruh*
Tra'os   TRAY*–us*
Vash'ti   VASH*–tee*
Zac–che'us   *zack–*KEY*–us*
Zar'e–phath   ZARE*–eh–fath*
Zeb'e–dee   ZEB*–uh–dee*
Ze–rub'ba–bel   *zeh–*ROOB*–bah–bell*
Zip–po'rah   *zip–*POH*–ruh*